The Practical Helps Library™

President Trump And The Q Movement Versus Satan And The Deep State

Roger Henri Trepanier

© 2019

This book is dedicated to President Donald John Trump, who left a very successful career as a businessman to take on the most difficult job in the world, and that without remuneration; in order to expose, bring to justice, and clean up a corrupt and evil Deep State that was intent on destroying the United States as a free Constitutional Republic!

Titles available from Roger Henri Trepanier in The Truth Seeker's Library™ series:

God Did Not Create Human Beings To Die… But To Live On… Eternally!

Finding Comfort And Encouragement In The Promises Of God In The Last Days

How We Know For Sure That We Are Living In The Last Days!

Have You Ever Wondered What Happens After Death?

An Introduction To The New World That Is Coming On The Earth

Deeper Truths Of The Christian Life

Evangelism As God Intended

Keeping On Serving God In The Last Days

The Mysterious World Of Angels And Demons

No One Loves As He Loves!

Thanks Be To God For His Indescribable Gift!

The Church Is Very Much Alive, Well, And Growing!

Tracing The Steps Of The Son Of God From Eternity To Eternity!

War, And Going To War, Is Simply Not Of God!

God Never Meant Prayer To Be A Mystery!

Health Is One Of God's Great Blessings!

Removing The Mystery Surrounding Baptism!

This World's Return To Paganism Is Almost Complete!

Removing The Mystery Surrounding Heaven!

God's Covenants Were Meant For Mankind's Blessing!

Titles available from Roger Henri Trepanier in The Practical Helps Library™ series:

Learning to Overcome The Perplexities Of This Present Life

So, I Hear You Want To Work With Seniors?

I Will Not Have This Man To Rule Over Me!

Spiritual Truth To Warm The Heart!

Fasten Your Seatbelts: Turbulence Ahead!

Living A Normal Christian Life In An Increasingly Abnormal World!

If You Have Jesus; You Do Not Need Drugs!

To Do God's Will Is To Have A Foretaste Of Heaven!
This World Is Ready For The Rule Of The Antichrist!

**Titles available from Roger Henri Trepanier
in The Christian Fiction Library™ series:**

The Beginning Of A New Dawn
It Is Never Too Late For Love!
The True To Life Musings Of Fred And Ernie
Between A Rock And A Hard Place!
Love Knows No Boundaries!
A Woman Worth Pursuing!
Love Is More Than Just A Four Letter Word!
The Twists And Turns Of The Life Of Faith!

**Titles available from Roger Henri Trepanier
in The Word Of God Library™ series:**

God's First Letter To The Thessalonians
God's Second Letter To The Thessalonians
God's Letter To Believers Through Jude
God's Three Short Letters To Believers Through John
God's Letter To Scattered Believers Through James
God's Letter To Titus
God's Prophetic Word To Mankind Through Daniel

INTRODUCTION

There is at the present time a battle raging, both in the physical and spiritual realms, for the souls and minds of human beings, which is worldwide in scope. The first salvo of that battle was launched on June 16, 2015, when Donald John Trump announced his candidacy for President of the United States. As we will see from the book, Mr Trump did not set out to become President per se, in terms of needing fame or fortune or power, for he already had all that, without all the headaches that always comes from holding public office, and especially the Presidency of the United States, without doubt the most demanding job in the world.

When Mr Trump put his hat in the ring, he was already well aware of the condition of his country of birth, and knew many of the reasons for its slide from being leader of the free world toward becoming a third world banana republic. So his candidacy was intended to put a stop to the people and forces that were at work to bring the demise of the United States, which will be seen to be the Deep State! What this means then is that the battle is real, for on the one hand, President Trump is exposing the Deep State as to all its illegal and evil activities, which the Deep State does not want the public to become knowledgeable of.

What this book seeks to do then is to present information in the hope that it will open the eyes of those who are not yet awake to what is truly going on in the world, as made known by President Trump and the Q team; for as will be shown very few things are as they seem! The present days that we are living in are definitely not in accordance with the saying, 'what you see is what you get!' If there is one thing to characterize the age we are presently in it is one of deception! White is no longer white, and black is no longer black, but myriad shades in between, all designed to confuse and undermine what God has instituted. The foundations we all depended on since the beginning of time are crumbling before our eyes. People are starting to question whether this world makes sense anymore. It is at such a time as this that God has seen fit to drop President Trump and the Q movement into our midst, as will be shown to be the case from this book.

And the funny thing is that I had no plans to write a book on President Trump, the Q movement, Satan, and the Deep State, for the simple reason that one of my books published last year was titled, "The World Is Ready For The Rule Of The Antichrist!," in which I had one very long chapter dealing with the Presidencies of Obama and of Trump, in relation to the coming rule of the antichrist over a one world government, with all signs pointing to that event being close at hand. However – and this is important – I was not at all aware at that time of Q and the Q movement! I only became aware of Q and the Q movement about a week after that book was published.

Since that time, my eyes have been opened to so much more of what is going on in the world, which has only served to heighten my belief that we are even closer to the second coming from Heaven to earth of God's Son, The Lord Jesus Christ, to remove the believers from the earth in order to bring in His judgment on the unbelievers of this world. And since I have been a believer for almost forty years, I was enabled of God to see many parallels in the Q movement to what God said it would be like in the last days of the present age. And God further made His servant aware of many pitfalls that believers could be led astray by in all of this, which is no doubt one more reason for why He has now led His servant to write this book.

And I have to confess my bias at the outset in that I have been closely following President Trump since he announced his candidacy. My reason for doing so was due to knowing even before Obama had been elected President that the man was a fraud and should never have been elected President in the first place. On the night he was elected, my first reaction was to say to others that the country would be going downhill from that moment onward, and would never be the same. As we will see from the book, Obama was a puppet of the Deep State and their globalist agenda, and was working in accordance with a 16 year plan to bring down the USA, with his tenure being for eight years, with the final eight years of that sixteen year plan being left up for Hillary Clinton to complete. But, as we all know by now, that did not happen. And thank God for that!

What many believers are aware of is that the election of President Trump was a definite intervention of God at this time in world history. But one of the questions we need to ask is: But for how long? For the reality is that in accordance with what God has made known to us in His word (and as we will see in Chapter Three of the book), there is an antichrist coming on the world stage to rule over a one world government. That is a given, simply because God said that is what will happen! So for how long then will God put off that event, which He is presently doing on a worldwide scale through President Trump, Q, and the Q movement?

Then as to the book itself, we are to note that it has been divided into three sections. The first section is titled, "The main characters," and has chapters dealing with President Trump, Q and the Q movement, Satan, the devil, and the Deep State, as the four main characters on the world stage at this time. The second section is titled, "Important perspectives to be aware of" and deals with what is happening in plain sight in the physical realm and also as what can be applied as part of the spiritual world around us. And then the third and final section is titled, "Things for believers to guard against and to do." As an evangelist, I do care not only for the salvation of precious souls, but also deeply care for my brothers and sisters who are also believers in The Lord Jesus Christ. At a time such as this, I do not want any of them to be led astray by all the confusion and deception that is evident in all spheres of life at this present time!

Then we are to note that at the back of the book there is an Addenda with four sections. In Addendum A, there is a brief outline of the four ages of time, for any reading the book that might not be aware of the fact that God has divided all of time into four ages. Then in Addendum B, there is a brief outline of the two comings from Heaven to earth in time of God's Son,

The Lord Jesus Christ, for any who may not be familiar with this information either. In Addendum C, we have a presentation of the gospel, which is the good news that God gives in His word regarding His Son, The Lord Jesus Christ, for any readers who might not as yet have that vital personal relationship with God through faith in His Son. And then in Addendum D, under 'Useful resources,' we have the video links referenced in the book.

And before closing this Introduction, we should mention a few words of a personal nature, since we are all somewhat curious human beings. So after completing 21 years of formal education and then spending almost 28 years working in Project Engineering and Management in the Corporate offices of a large utility, God called His servant as a non-denominational evangelist in early 1999, and then sent him out more than two thousand miles away from family and friends, to the place of service God has assigned, which is where His servant has been, and is still serving Him, as evangelist, counselor, and author. God's servant is a widower with three adopted children, all now married with a family of their own.

Please note the two websites listed below, which have been established for the purpose of interacting with readers and also for gospel ministry:

http://www.pilgrimpathwaypublications.com

http://servantofmosthigh.com

And now my prayer is that God will richly bless you as you read this book, and greatly minister to every need in your life, as only God can! To Him be all praise, honor, and glory, with thanksgiving, both now and forevermore! Amen.

CONTENTS

Page

Introduction

**President Trump And The Q Movement Versus Satan
And The Deep State**

SECTION ONE
THE MAIN CHARACTERS

"…For there is no authority except from God, and those which exist are established by God."

Romans 13:1 in part

CHAPTER ONE

President Donald J Trump

Whether one likes, loves, hates, or is indifferent to the man, the reality is that there are certain undeniable facts that we should be aware of about Donald John Trump, who became the 45th President of the United States on January 20, 2017. One of those facts is that on inauguration day, he was the oldest man to ever serve the office of President, being 70 years of age. Another fact is that he was the wealthiest person ever to serve in that position, being a multi-billionaire at the time of his election. Then a third fact is that President Trump is the first man to ever serve in the office without ever having held political office of any kind, or to have ever served in the US military. President Trump had been a very successful businessman before his election to office, with multiple hats, namely as developer, television producer, and author, to name just a few.

Another undeniable fact about President Trump is that he came to power on a campaign promise in the form of a slogan, which was to 'Make America Great Again' (MAGA). So what we need to be aware of here, which is critical, is that in order to make America great again, Trump had to undo all the damage that Obama had purposely done to weaken the United States, both economically and militarily, while in office. And one will not understand this last statement here unless one is aware that while Obama was a GLOBALIST – seeking with other globalists to see a one world government established, through all countries setting aside their sovereignty, while adopting open borders with unrestricted immigrant flow – Trump on the other hand was unabashed from the beginning in letting the country and the world know that he was a NATIONALIST, which is opposite to a globalist, in terms of being for a sovereign state, with secure borders, and a restriction on immigration! A very important short video that the Trump campaign put out in 2016 should be watched at this point, where candidate Trump laid out the agenda that was needed in the US at this time, and which resonated with voters: https://www.youtube.com/watch?v=G2qIXXafxCQ

Therefore, from a geopolitical and strategic aspect, Obama's eight years in office must be seen as his attempt to weaken the United States, since all globalists know that for a one world government to succeed, the United States' role as the leader of the free world must be greatly diminished in every way possible. And this Obama proceeded to do from within – financially, diplomatically, militarily, morally, and socially. It is clear that with his godless agenda, Obama was sure to divide Americans, between the right and the left; between the religious and the non-religious, between black and white, and in this way fuel the fire of widespread hatred leading to anarchy, as a perfect setting for the setting up of a one world government!

It is obvious to the objective observer that the Obama administration excelled in this through its lack of border control of illegal immigrants coming into the country during his term of office, even signing executive orders to give these illegal immigrants legal status. At the same time, the Obama administration promoted world-encompassing agreements during his tenure, such at the Paris Climate Change Agreement, which for the first time in history brought all the nations of the world into one agreement, committing each nation to fight climate change. And then there was the infamous Trans Pacific Partnership (TPP), which was the centerpiece of Obama's strategic push to Asia, which upon its creation on October 15, 2015, became the largest trading block in the world, commanding forty percent of world trade. And then there was the equally infamous Iran deal. What all these had in common was that none benefited the United States as a country, or its workers!

So the first order of business that President Trump sought to accomplish was to place the United States on a solid footing economically again, for without the wealth, not much else can be carried out, which therefore meant that the first thing to go were all the regulations that Obama had brought in to weaken the United States economically. Then Trump proceeded to greatly build up the US militarily again, which has been the dominant military power in the world since WW1. As we begin 2019, the United States is once again the acknowledged sole superpower in the world. Here is a video on this fact: https://www.youtube.com/watch?v=zCqKnqMqIhI

The Trump administration also took steps to build a wall at the southern border with Mexico in a further attempt to stem the tide of illegal immigrants, coupled with the accompanying flow of illegal drugs and human traffickers; while going about removing all the Obama sponsored programs to prevent giving persons here illegally legal status and access to benefits, including seeking to end federally funded sanctuary cities for illegals. But we need to realize that there were a lot of globalists that got entrenched at all levels of society and the government during Obama's tenure. And while the Democratic Party is funded by globalists, such as George Soros (whom we will talk about in Chapter Four), nevertheless there are also many Republican globalists, both in the House and Senate, which means a lot of never-Trumpers, who stand opposed to Trump's agenda, although some of these have now resigned, died, or lost their seats in the recent midterm elections.

The Trump administration then further moved to bring in tariffs and redo trade agreements that were not in the best interest of the United States, such as NAFTA (North America Free Trade Agreement). During the Obama years, more than 10,000 companies had left the United States to set up shop elsewhere, with many of these going to China, which allowed these companies in only on the condition that they share their technology with the Chinese, which the Chinese then used to set up clone products to compete directly with those US companies, in effect stealing intellectual property through their unfair policies and practices! As a result of actions by the Trump administration, many of these companies are returning to the US, especially with the introduction of massive tax cuts, for both individuals and companies, with the result that the US manufacturing sector is booming again, as well as the small business sector, which had been strangled with overbearing regulations.

Another very important fact about President Trump is that he has been the most pro-evangelical President so far, and the greatest advocate and protector of the state of Israel in US history, removing – through legislation and executive orders – every stumbling block that Obama had placed in the path of Christians to freely practice their faith and for Israel to defend itself. President Trump also finally formally recognized Jerusalem as the capital of Israel and moved the US embassy there. At the same time, President Trump has been seeking to prevent Islamic terrorist inroads into the United States by preventing immigration from those Muslim nations that were sponsors of Islamic terrorism.

So the short of it is that at the time of writing, the United States, in two years under a Trump Presidency, has reestablished itself as the leader of the free world, being back now on a solid footing both economically and militarily. At the same time, Trump advised global organizations, such as the UN (United Nations), that they needed to change; for one thing, by no longer being the bashing ground for denouncing Israel at every turn; and also telling the nations comprising NATO (North Atlantic Treaty Organization) – which had been established after WW2 to keep the Soviets in check, while at the same time establishing a US presence in Europe in order to protect it – that they needed to pay their fair share of the costs for their security. And what many patriots were glad to see about President Trump was that he not only campaigned as an avowed nationalist, not only intent on restoring the United States to superpower status both economically and militarily, but also in restoring the power to the people, meaning the states, instead of power being concentrated in a federal government.

What is fairly obvious from all of this then is that we have been given a respite by God (that is, a pause) from our slide into darkness of the pit of hell that Obama, as a globalist seeking a one world government, had allowed the United States and the world to slide into, which would have made it easier for a one world government to be established once the United States had been weakened, as it had been during his Presidency. Now with Trump re-establishing the US as a strong leader of the free world, which means not only keeping the world's shipping lanes open, but also keeping rogue nations and regimes in check throughout the world, means that the globalist agenda is being restrained in some measure at the moment. So we come again to the question of why would God allow this? And for how long?

Since it is also an undeniable fact that God is Almighty and the only Sovereign over all His creation, from the beginning to the end, while also working in accordance with a plan for the four ages of time, then this means that President Trump's coming to power at this time in history was no coincidence, but rather is to be seen as allowed of God, or else he never would have become President. By the way, this also applies to every other President before him, even Barrack Obama! As the Bible verse says as a quote preceding this chapter, those in authority have been established by God, whether we readily accept or even understand that truth.

And we cannot forget the fact that those whom God does allow to come to power are there only to serve God's purposes, which He is outworking through the four ages of time, which covers all of human history on earth, whether these leaders realize this or not. And so, what is perhaps the most heartening of all to believers, as this is being written, is that President Trump has restored God to His rightful place as true head of nations, including the USA, with President Trump often acknowledging that fact at his rallies and at his cabinet meetings, which all begin with prayer in Jesus' Name!

It is no wonder then that the largest block of his supporters consists of evangelical believers. For what we also need to be aware of is that a majority of federal employees voted for

Hillary Clinton in the 2016 Presidential Election. According to an independent Government Business Council/GovExec.com poll released on January 18, 2017, 62 percent of respondents chose Clinton compared to 28 percent who voted for Donald Trump, which means that there is a lot of possible resistance that was left behind in the federal bureaucracy from eight years of the Obama Presidency.

And now as we pass the two year mark of President Trump's first term, he has been seen as being a true friend of the average person, by putting Americans to work again, and raising their standard of living, by bringing especially manufacturing jobs back to the US. And so, we will end this first chapter with a partial list of the accomplishments of President Trump and his Administration in his two years in office so far. And the reason this is being done here is simply to show that those who oppose President Trump do so due to an ideological bias that comes from having an opposing agenda, and not at all based on honesty, as will be crystal clear as we continue on in the book!

And so, here is a partial list of the Trump Administration accomplishments for 2017, 2018 (the full list can be seen on the Whitehouse website at https://www.whitehouse.gov (with all such links also appearing under 'Useful Resources' in Appendix D in the order in which they appear in the book):

- Almost 4 million jobs created since the election.
- More Americans are now employed than ever recorded before in our history.
- More than 400,000 manufacturing jobs created since the election.
- Economic growth hit 4.2 percent last quarter.
- New unemployment claims hit a 49-year low.
- Median household income has hit highest level ever recorded.
- African-American unemployment has achieved the lowest rate ever recorded.
- Hispanic-American unemployment is at the lowest rate ever recorded.

- Asian-American unemployment achieved the lowest rate ever recorded.
- Women's unemployment reached the lowest rate in 65 years.
- Youth unemployment has hit the lowest rate in nearly half a century.
- Lowest unemployment rate ever recorded for Americans without a high school diploma.
- Veterans' unemployment reached its lowest rate in nearly 20 years.
- Almost 3.9 million Americans have been lifted off food stamps since the election.
- The Pledge to America's Workers has resulted in employers committing to train more than 4 million Americans.
- 95 percent of U.S. manufacturers are optimistic about the future — the highest ever.
- Retail sales up 6 percent ending 2018 over the previous year.
- The biggest package of tax cuts and reforms in history.
- As a result of the tax bill, small businesses will have the lowest top marginal tax rate in more than 80 years.
- Opened ANWR and approved Keystone XL and Dakota Access Pipelines.
- Record number of regulations eliminated.
- Enacted regulatory relief for community banks and credit unions.
- Obamacare individual mandate penalty GONE.
- More affordable healthcare options are being provided through association health plans and short-term duration plans.
- The FDA has now approved more affordable generic drugs than ever before in history and many drug companies are freezing or reversing planned price increases.
- Provided $6 billion in NEW funding to fight the opioids epidemic.
- Cancelled the illegal, anti-coal, so-called Clean Power Plan.
- Increased our coal exports by 60 percent and U.S. oil production recently reached an all-time high.

- The United States is now a net natural gas exporter for the first time since 1957.

- Withdrew from the job-killing Paris Climate Accord.

- Secured record $700 billion in military funding for 2018; $716 billion next year.

- NATO allies are spending $69 billion more on defense since 2016.

- Process has begun to make the Space Force the 6th branch of the Armed Forces.

- Confirmed more circuit court judges than any other new administration.
Confirmed Supreme Court Justice Neil Gorsuch and Brett Kavanaugh.

- Withdrew from the horrible, one-sided Iran Deal.

- Moved U.S. Embassy to Jerusalem.

- Protecting Americans from terrorists with the Travel Ban, upheld by Supreme Court.

- Concluded a historic U.S.- Mexico - Canada Trade Deal to replace NAFTA.

- Reached a breakthrough agreement with the E.U. to increase U.S. exports.

- Imposed tariffs on foreign steel and aluminum to protect our national security.

- Imposed tariffs on China in response to China's forced technology transfer, intellectual property theft, and their abusive trade practices.

- Net exports are on track to increase by $59 billion this year.

- Improved vetting and screening for refugees, and switched focus to overseas resettlement.

- We have begun BUILDING THE WALL. Republicans want STRONG BORDERS and NO CRIME. Democrats want OPEN BORDERS which equals MASSIVE CRIME.

"For nothing is hidden that will not become evident, nor anything secret that will not be known and come to light."

Luke 8:17

CHAPTER TWO

Q and the Q movement

1) Why Q became necessary

President Trump came to power on January 20, 2017, and by the fall of 2017 it had become clear to him and his administration, and also to his supporters, that all the mainstream media (such as CNN, ABC, CBS, NBC, MSNBC, the Washington Post, The New York Times, etc.) was not going to give the average American accurate news about what the Trump Administration was achieving on their behalf, since these media companies were ALL supporting Hillary Clinton in the 2016 Presidential election, and ALL expected her to win.

And to make matters worse, social media platforms (such as Twitter, Facebook, YouTube, Google, etc.), which had been suppressing, or eliminating, conservative thought from their sites during the Obama years, now increased that suppression even more on their platforms, even extending it to Trump supporters. What this meant then is that an ALTERNATIVE SOURCE OF NEWS DECIMATION was needed by the Trump administration, if President Trump was going to keep his supporters informed as to the truth of what his administration was doing, in terms of fulfilling all campaign promises.

And so, this was one primary reason why Q came to be; namely to be a means of reaching supporters with the news, which had not been compromised by a mainstream media that was part of the Deep State standing in opposition to President Trump's MAGA addenda. Then the Q movement naturally developed as people became aware of the information provided by Q and started relying on it as a credible source of news. And as people had their eyes opened to what was really going on, they became Q followers.

But there was another important reason for Q as a source of information for Trump supporters, which was to expose the Deep State for what it really was, as not only corrupt through and through, but also as being evil beyond imagination, as will be seen in Chapter Four. So that is why the mainstream media, which is part of the Deep State, tries to suppress the truth about Q and the Q movement by painting it as a far rightwing conspiracy theory! They do not want awakened citizen, but rather sheep that they can control.

2) So what is Q?

An obvious question that then comes up is: What is Q? The answer that is widely held in the Q movement is that Q consists of a team of military and civilian personnel close to, and including, President Trump, who have the very highest clearances on all the intelligence available to the United States, spanning not only the whole of the United States' history, but also every other country on earth, including all persons of interest and in any position of power. In other words, if there are any dark secrets out there, this group has knowledge of it. If one is not convinced of this, then one will be after following Q for a while, simply based on the depth and scope of the sensitive information being provided by the Q team.

3) Where does one get the information provided by the Q team?

The Q team (which will henceforth only be referred to as Q) started posting detailed information on an anonymous channel called '4chan' on October 28, 2017; but soon afterwards moved to another anonymous channel called '8chan,' due to security concerns. The Secret Service, which protects President Trump, is also now providing the security of this platform. As of today (March 16, 2019) there have been 3096 posts by Q to 8 chan. These posts can be viewed by anyone with a computer, or any other device connected to the internet, by going to https://qmap.pub. (before seeking to go to this site, please see note to readers below)

(Note to readers inserted here September 12, 2020

As one can understand, as we get closer to the November 3rd Presidential elections, the Deep State is working overtime to take down all sites associated with President Trump, which includes the Q movement. As a result, the website qmap.pub was taken down this past week. No one knows when, or if it will be back up again. Therefore, the information in the paragraph below this note will not apply until it is back up again. In the meantime, Q posts are available at the following sites:

https://qalerts.app/

https://qagg.news/

https://qanon.pub/

https://qanon.news/Q/

Let us remember that there is information warfare going on!)

If one looks at the Qmap on this website, one can not only see every post by Q in sequential numerical order since October 28, 2017, but one can also find a lot of useful information on the left sidebar. It is highly recommended that one begin with the second and third tabs on the left sidebar, which detail the major players and the major themes that have been identified by Q in the Q posts (to go from looking at the sidebar back t the Q posts, just click on the 'Q' in the top left corner). One other very useful tool on the Qmap is the 'search' function, where one can search any subject one is interested in, with all Q posts associated with that subject being then listed in numerical order, from the earliest to the latest (and to return to the current Q posts again, just click on the green reset button to the top far right). Another useful tool at the top is a listing of all President Trump's tweets on Twitter, starting with the most recent. To activate, one only needs to hit the 'Potus off' button (and the reset button again to return to the Q posts).

4) How does one go about deciphering the Q posts?

As can be expected, thousands of channels on YouTube, and other platforms (such as Twitter, Facebook, Gab, BitChute, etc.), including personal websites, have sprung up in order to provide Trump supporters, often referred to as 'patriots,' some DECIPHERING OF THE INFORMATION PROVIDED BY Q in the Q drops on 8chan, or to provide news updates relating to past or current Q posts; for it must be realized that Q does not necessarily post every day; only when there is relevant information to be shared.

Apart from those already mentioned, there are also many resources that have since sprung up to help the Q movement patriots – which now number in the millions worldwide – since Q encourages each person following the Q posts to do their own research. For instance, there are also 'anons,' which stands for 'anonymous persons', who are advanced researchers outside the Q team that provide assistance to the Q movement in deciphering and better understanding the Q posts, since these are sometimes given in military code and/or abbreviations. If one clicks on the title of any of the Q posts, one will be brought to the Q research board, where the anons have posted their information, which is also on 8chan, which means that this information is also then protected by the Secret Service. One can also reach the Q research board at the following link: https://8ch.net/qresearch/index.html.

5) Suggested YouTube channels, since one needs to beware of Deep State infiltration

What needs to be remembered here is that there is an epic open battle for all to see that is going on, not only in the United States, but also worldwide, between President Trump, the Q team and the Q movement on the one hand, versus the Deep State on the other, for the simple reason that President Trump and the Q team have ALL the information required to bring down the Deep State, and has been making that information public since the first Q post has been made on October 28, 2017. What this means then is that the Deep State also has access to the Q posts and has therefore set up many websites and channels on various platforms in an effort to not only misinform the Q patriots, but also to divide them. For this reason, links to two credible sites have been provided here to help the beginner. One can then go on to discover one's favorites. So the first is the X22 Report, at: https://www.youtube.com/user/X22Report/videos?app=deskt op, and the second is In Pursuit Of The Truth, IPOT for short: https://www.youtube.com/channel/UCAyrKoW31y5UcsRjh2lt vxQ/videos.

6) Examples of some Q posts

What would prove useful at this point is to actually reproduce an early Q post from Q, and then a recent one, in order to give the reader a firsthand look at the Q posts while we are speaking of them. And so, for an earlier one, let us look at Q post #73 from November 4, 2017:

POTUS Twitter Attack 73
Anonymous 4 Nov 2017 - 6:22:08 PM
What was POTUS' last Tweet (prior to)?
To who was it addressed?
When was POTUS' Twitter taken down?
Why is this relevant?
What was POTUS' last Tweet (prior to)?
Who was it addressed to specifically?
When was POTUS' Twitter taken down?
Has this ever happened before?
Why now?
Coincidence?
How many times did the attack occur (secondary clean up)?
What is the purpose of tracking?
What is the purpose of disruption?
Why did POTUS have military guards (uniform) while in HI?
Why is this relevant?

Do military guards (uniform) typically assist the USSS?
Why is this relevant?
What flying object was recently shot down?
Why is this relevant?
How precise is geo tracking (non-public c-level pro)?
Why is this relevant?
Alice & Wonderland.
Q

Please note the post title at the top and the post number to the right of the title, then noting that it is anonymous content, followed by the Q post itself, usually in the form of questions, which are designed to make one think, and also do personal research. Now let us note a more recent Q post, which is post #2816 from February 19, 2019:

WE ALL WANT TO SEE EQUAL JUSTICE UNDER THE LAW 2816

Q !!mG7VJxZNCI 19 Feb 2019 - 4:43:38 PM
The DECLASSIFICATION of all requested documents (+ more) will occur.
This is not a game.
Do not let personal (emotional) desires ("do it now""now""what is taking so long""NOW!") take over.
Logical thinking and strategy should always be applied.
Game-Theory.
WE ALL WANT TO SEE EQUAL JUSTICE UNDER THE LAW.
NEW THREATS (investigations by [SDNY], [AS], [MW] in an effort to delay/prevent release ('insurance extension') WILL FAIL.
TRANSPARENCY is the only way forward.
Define the following:
Treason.
Sedition.
Subversion.
Conspiracy to commit...

Do you understand and fully appreciate the GRAVITY of the situation?

Do you understand and fully appreciate what POTUS endures each and every singly day?

He loves this County.

He loves you.

WE MUST STAND TOGETHER IN THIS FIGHT.

There is EVIL in this world.

There is DARKNESS in this world.

There are those in POWER who wish to CONTROL (enslave) you.

To keep you sedated.

To keep you unaware.

To keep you blind.

This will be on our timetable.

(….AND WE WILL DELIVER).

(Transparency and Prosecution)

There is simply no other way.

[Except 1]

Q

In this post, we see that Q does not ask as many questions, wanting instead to provide information and encouragement to Q movement patriots. And please note that sometimes there are errors, such as 'singly' instead of 'single,' and 'county' instead of 'country.' Sometimes these are corrected in a follow up post, but sometimes they are not, being intentional in order to convey some coded message. In this case this was partially corrected the next day.

7) Do not be surprised by the constant references to God

What should not surprise anyone are the occasional references to God and the Bible in the Q posts. We need to remember that on inauguration day, half of President Trump's cabinet was made up of evangelical Christians, with Vice President Pence and his wife also being evangelical Christians. President Trump even has a council made up of selected evangelical ministers, who are there to provide him with counsel. And let us not forget that President Trump largest block of supporters is made up of Bible-believing Christians. Therefore, it should be expected that there are likely some Bible-believing Christians among those on the Q team, and that the Q posts themselves often have a reference to God, or to the Bible. Let us note three examples of this in the Q posts, the first one being post #54 on November 2, 2017:

Jeremiah 29:11 54

Anonymous 2 Nov 2017 - 12:39:41 PM

"For I know the plans I have for you," declares the LORD, "plans to prosper you and not to harm you, plans to give you hope and a future."

Then let us notice also Q post #1432 from May 20, 2018:

Be Strong in the Lord and in His Mighty Power 1432

Q !CbboFOtcZs 20 May 2018 - 4:34:26 PM

"Finally, be strong in the Lord and in his mighty power. Put on the full armor of God so that you can take your stand against the devil's schemes. For our struggle is not against flesh and blood, but against the rulers, against the authorities, against the powers of this dark world and against the spiritual forces of evil in the heavenly realms. Therefore put on the full armor of God, so that when the day of evil comes, you may be able to stand your ground, and after you have done everything, to stand. Stand firm then, with the belt of truth buckled around your waist, with the breastplate of righteousness in place, and with your feet fitted with the readiness that comes from the gospel of peace. In addition to all this, take up the shield of faith, with which you can extinguish all the flaming arrows of the evil one. Take the helmet of salvation and the sword of the Spirit, which is the word of God. And pray in the Spirit on all occasions with all kinds of prayers and requests. With this in mind, be alert and always keep on praying for all the saints."

– Ephesians 6:10-18

And there was also Q post #2744 from February 16, 2019:

Q Quotes the Bible (2 Thessalonians 3:3, Psalm 46:1, Matthew 6:13) 2744

Q!!mG7VJxZNCI 16 Feb 2019 - 7:46:28 PM

"But the Lord is faithful, and he will strengthen you and protect you from the evil one." - 2 Thessalonians 3:3

"God is our refuge and strength, an ever-present help in trouble." - Psalm 46:1

"And lead us not into temptation, but deliver us from the evil one." - Matthew 6:13

Q

And so, as we close this chapter on Q and the Q movement, it must be realized that as a result of all the resistance to President Trump and his administration from the Deep State, which has become entrenched literally everywhere, his OFFICIAL CHANNELS OF COMMUNICATION WITH HIS SUPPORTERS has been, since October 28, 2017, THE Q POSTS, PLUS PRESIDENT TRUMP'S TWEETS ON TWITTER, PLUS THE INFORMATION PROVIDED ON THE WHITEHOUSE WEBSITE, at https://www.whitehouse.gov/, AND ALSO PRESIDENT TRUMP'S PERSONAL WEBSITE at https://www.donaldjtrump.com.

And one last thought to keep in mind, which is that the Q movement has now gone worldwide, with many YouTube channels and websites having been set up in the English speaking world, such as in the UK, Europe, Australia, and Canada, which are all deciphering Q posts for their own national audiences. And even the YELLOW VEST movement in France and around the world is to be seen as also being an offshoot of the Q movement, in that those taking part are doing so in an attempt to register their opposition to the Deep State in their own countries.

"For our struggle is not against flesh and blood, but against the rulers, against the powers, against the world forces of this darkness, against the spiritual forces of wickedness in the heavenly places."

Ephesians 6:12

CHAPTER THREE

Satan, the devil

The only One who knows the full history of this sinister and evil character, known as Satan the devil, is God. What this means then is that all the information that we have of him is only what God has provided in His word, the Bible. So what we will do in this chapter is look at what God has revealed since the beginning of creation and throughout the four ages of time regarding the devil, whose name is Satan, for the express purpose of then being able to understand the Deep State. In other words, we cannot even come close to understanding what the Deep State is, and what it is about, without first having a good grasp as to who the devil is and what he is seeking to accomplish during the four ages of time! For what the devil, who is evil personified, is attempting to do in time, is to oppose and counterfeit all that God, Who is good, plans to do, as made known in His word. And so, the devil accomplishes all his evil work in time through his demons (who are fallen angels) in the spiritual realm and also through those human beings who are part of the Deep State in this physical world of ours!

1) The first age begins with God's perfect original creation, where He makes known to mankind what He requires of him

Before we begin our look at Satan, the devil, and in order to later understand what the Deep State is, we first need to note God's original creation at Genesis 1, which is when time began to be marked, which event also marked the beginning of the first age of time. And there we see that on the sixth day of creation – after God had finished bringing into existence all that is found in the physical and spiritual realms, which included human and angelic beings – God said at Genesis 1:31, "God saw all that He had made, and behold, it was very good. And there was evening and there was morning, the sixth day." What this means then is that there was no sin, and therefore no evil, in all of God's perfect original creation. In other words, since God is Holy and Good and altogether Righteous, then this means that ALL was "very good," which included the first man in the physical realm of earth, Adam, from whom we are all descended as a human race; and also included all the angelic beings in the spiritual realm.

And what is very important to note for our present purpose of what God requires of His human creation on earth, we are to now note what God said at Genesis 1:27,28, "[27] God created man in His own image, in the image of God He created him; male and female He created them. [28] God blessed them; and God said to them, "BE FRUITFUL AND MULTIPLY, AND FILL THE EARTH, AND SUBDUE IT, AND RULE OVER the fish of the sea and over the birds of the sky and over EVERY LIVING THING THAT MOVES ON THE EARTH." So there are two very important truths we need to note from this for our present purpose. The first is that God's order to mankind is to "be fruitful and multiply..." In other words, as male and female, have children and increase on the earth. Then secondly, God clearly gives the rule to mankind over all his non-human living creatures on earth. In other words, it is to mankind that God originally gave the rule over the earth to, with man having that rule as under God.

Then when we turn to Genesis 2, we see God look at that original creation again and now adds much greater detail. And so at Genesis 2:7 we see that God made Adam, the first man, with three constituent parts, that being a body, a spirit, and a soul (also noting 1 Thessalonians 5:23). And what we need to keep in mind about these three constituent parts of man here is that only the body dies physically, which is but an enclosing shell for the spirit and the soul, which go on to exist forever once brought into existence by God. The human spirit

40

is that part of us that God made so that we might interact with Him, since He is spirit (noting John 4:24) and made us in His image for that purpose. The soul is the human part of us that enables to interact with other souls, that is, other human beings.

And then let us note for our present purpose what God does at Genesis 2:22 when He gives us greater detail of how Eve was brought into existence by God, and then tells us at Genesis 2:24 what His will was for the man and the woman, "[22] The Lord God fashioned into a woman the rib which He had taken from the man, AND BROUGHT HER TO THE MAN... [24] For this reason a man shall leave his father and his mother, AND BE JOINED TO HIS WIFE; AND THEY SHALL BECOME ONE FLESH." In other words, here we see God institute marriage, so that it would be within the confines of marriage that the man and the woman (as Adam and Eve, and not Adam and Steve; nor Eve and Helen) were to have the sexual union in order to multiply and increase on the earth. That sexual union had as its primary aim the bringing of children into the world by means of a married man and woman; although we see later from 1 Corinthians 7:2-5 that the sexual union between husband and wife in marriage was also for the satisfaction of the sexual needs of the couple.

Then lastly, in regards to what God made known in regards to what He requires of mankind when first created at that original creation, let us note that at Genesis 2:8,15-17, we there read, "The Lord God planted a garden toward the east, in Eden; and there He placed the man whom He had formed... [15] Then the Lord God took the man and put him into the garden of Eden TO CULTIVATE IT AND KEEP IT. [16] THE LORD GOD COMMANDED THE MAN, SAYING, "FROM ANY TREE OF THE GARDEN YOU MAY EAT FREELY; [17] BUT FROM THE TREE OF THE KNOWLEDGE OF GOOD AND EVIL YOU SHALL NOT EAT, FOR IN THE DAY THAT YOU EAT FROM IT YOU WILL SURELY DIE.."

So we see God not only give Adam work to do for Him in the garden of Eden here on earth, but that this was also to be a place of testing. In other words, so far Adam was innocent, meaning that he knew not good or evil, not yet knowing sin. So God gives Adam a command here, as to what he is to do and what he is NOT to do. This meant that Adam had a choice for the first time, which was to OBEY God, or to DISOBEY God by taking from the forbidden tree. And God was clear as to what the outcome would be if Adam disobeyed God; in that it would mean death, both in its physical and in its spiritual aspect. Physical death meant that his body would one day die; and spiritual death meant that he would one day experience eternal separation from God, if before physical death he had not been forgiven of his sins by God and obtained eternal life from Him in salvation (as we shall later see).

And now we know what God requires of man, which was to live in accordance with God's word! In other words, what God was looking for from mankind was dependence on Him for all of one's needs and to live in obedience to his word out of love for Him! This is now where we see Adam and Eve being left by God before they next experience another life-changing test!

2) The entry of the original sin into God's perfect and sinless creation

And while God is never the author of sin or of evil, nevertheless, we are now to see that He allowed sin to enter His perfect and sinless human creation. We need to keep in mind that God Is not only Holy, that is without sin, but also Almighty, meaning He has unlimited power, and that He is also Sovereign, meaning that He is in absolute control of all that occurs during both time and eternity, since all that exists is only what was brought into existence by God, which is all designed to serve His purposes during the four ages of time and for all eternity to come! And this of course brings up the perennial question of why is there evil in the world, with the answer being that there is evil because of the presence of sin; which then brings up the additional question of why then did God allow sin to enter His perfect creation?

And the answer to that question has to do with the knowledge of good and evil. If God had not allowed sin, we would never have had evil, which means we would only have good, but with no experiential way to measure it, in the sense that we would not be able to comprehend it. What we must also realize here is that God is not only Holy, Almighty, and Sovereign, but He is also Good, Righteous, Loving, and Wise, to name just a few of His many attributes. What this means then is how would we know what good is without also knowing evil? Or how would we know what Holy truly means without there also being the unholy and profane; or how would we know what Righteous truly means apart from knowing what unrighteous is; or how would we know what Love truly is like without also knowing what hate is? And so sin was allowed by God, which also brought evil with it, in order that we might know that God is not only Good, but that we might also know and truly appreciate God in all the fullness of His attributes!

In other words, we know a thing due to its contrast. For instance, we have a better grasp of light from its opposite darkness. We can appreciate and enjoy a sunny day even more after having experienced a stormy day. And spring and summer are welcomed more after having experienced a cold winter with a lot of snow. Let us remember that God is also All-Knowing as well as All-Wise, which means that He knew what He was doing when He created this world and all that existed at first in its pristine state. We can be sure that God is working all things in accordance with a plan, which is for the blessing of His creatures and for His glory!

When time is no more, we will look back and exclaim what the apostle Paul did at Romans 11:33, when he was allowed to see God's workings with greater clarity, "Oh, the depth of the riches both of the wisdom and knowledge of God! How unsearchable are His judgments (that is, His decisions rendered) and unfathomable His ways!" Let us be clear on this, that because God is Perfect in every way possible, then no one can ever improve on all that God thinks, says, and does! What this means then is that He can be fully trusted, not only for this life, but for all eternity to come!

And so, the reality is that there came a day when sin entered God's perfect creation, and that day was when one of the angelic beings, who we will see was a cherub, actually sinned against God, which was the original sin to occur in God's perfect original creation, noting now what God tells us about that event, looking first at Isaiah 14:12-15, "[12] How you have fallen from heaven, O star of the morning (with this term "star of the morning" being "Hellel" in the original Hebrew, which means 'shining one'), son of the dawn! You have been cut down to the earth, you who have weakened the nations! [13] But YOU SAID IN YOUR HEART, 'I WILL ASCEND TO HEAVEN, I WILL RAISE MY THRONE ABOVE THE STARS OF GOD, and I will sit on the mount of assembly in the recesses of the north. [14] I will ascend above the heights of the clouds; I WILL MAKE MYSELF LIKE THE MOST HIGH.' [15] Nevertheless (says God) you will be thrust down to Sheol, to the recesses of the pit."

There are four things we need to know about this angelic being in view here, as "the star of the morning," or 'the shining one," which are: First, this angelic being could see God in that spiritual realm where he was, since angelic beings are spirit beings, and so is God, noting what He tells us of Himself at John 4:24, ""God is spirit, and those who worship Him must worship in spirit and truth." Secondly, we are to see that this angelic being had a number of desires, which he wanted to fulfill, so that five times we see him express those desires with the words, "I will...," which indicates that those desires came from himself and not from God. Let us note Psalm 103:20 here to see what God's desires were for the angelic beings that He had created, "Bless the Lord, you HIS ANGELS, mighty in strength, who perform His word, OBEYING THE VOICE OF HIS WORD!" And so we see from this that what God desired of the angelic beings when He created them was the same as what we have seen Him desire of mankind, which is to obey Him, not by doing one's own will, but rather by doing God's will. And just as it would be a sin for mankind to do one's own will instead of God's, and thereby disobey Him; therefore we are to see that it is also a sin here for this angelic being to be intent on carrying out one's own will instead of seeking to carry out God's will.

Then thirdly, we note that this angelic being is not content to just disobey God, but also has the stated goal of "I will make myself like the Most High." The phrase "make myself like" here is one word in the original Hebrew, that being "Damah," meaning to make himself like God is. In other words, we note here that this angelic being saw that God was ruling over all, when he mentions that "I will raise my throne," which speaks of one having the rule over others. Then the reference to "I will ascend to heaven" refers to the fact that he could see that this is where God dwelt as ruler. So what this indicates to us here is that this angelic being had no desire at all to obey God, that is, to serve Him by carrying out His will. Instead, he had made up his mind that he was going to be like God and have his own throne from which to rule over others, just like God did! So we see that PRIDE appears to be what made this angelic being sin against God, since we never see God give him a command, as we saw Him do with Adam at Genesis 2:16,17.

And then fourthly, we are to see that as a result of this sinful attitude and plans on the part of this angelic being, we see God pronounce judgment on him at verse 15, when He says, "Nevertheless you will be thrust down to Sheol, to the recesses of the pit." God had said to Adam, as a human being with a physical body, that the consequence of disobedience would be death; but in the case of this angelic being, since they do not die once created by God, but rather go on to exist eternally, this means that God only pronounces the sentence of this angelic being finding himself in the recesses of the pit of Sheol one day!

Sheol here in view is to be seen as a place below the surface of this present earth that God sets up as this angelic being sins against Him. A study of that subject also shows that there are three recesses or compartments in Sheol, which are to hold the souls and spirits of human beings after physical death and before the resurrection of the dead. Therefore, it is an intermediate place between the time of one's physical death and the time of one's resurrection from the dead, and will only exist in time until the final judgment of God, which is in view at Revelation 20:11-15 in God's word.

So what this means then is that in Sheol there is one compartment for the souls of deceased believers near the top, then a compartment for the souls and spirits of deceased unbelievers below that, then the pit, which is the lowest compartment of Sheol, closest to the fire of eventual hell that is already burning there, which God has lit due to sin; with that pit being reserved for this 'shining one' and the angelic beings that he subsequently also led into sin. Let us note what God later makes known at Deuteronomy 32:22 in part, of what would here apply, "For a fire is kindled in My anger, and burns to the lowest part of Sheol..." If there are any readers who would like to read more on the subject of death, angels, and demons, please see my books, "Have You Ever Wondered What Happens After Death?" and also "The Mysterious World Of Angels And Demons!"

Then the next very important passage of God's word that we need to look at is Ezekiel 28:13-17, where God further speaks again of this same angelic being, who committed the first sin to occur in His original sinless creation, there reading, "[13] You were in Eden, the garden of God; every precious stone was your covering: the ruby, the topaz and the diamond; the beryl, the onyx and the jasper; the lapis lazuli, the turquoise and the emerald; and the gold, the workmanship of your settings and sockets, was in you. ON THE DAY THAT YOU WERE CREATED they were prepared. [14] You were the anointed CHERUB who covers, and I (God) placed you there. You were on the holy mountain of God; you walked in the midst of the stones of fire. [15] YOU WERE BLAMELESS IN YOUR WAYS FROM THE DAY YOU WERE CREATED UNTIL UNRIGHTEOUSNESS WAS FOUND IN YOU. [16] By the abundance of your trade you were internally filled with violence, and YOU SINNED; therefore I have cast you as profane from the mountain of God. and I have destroyed you, O covering CHERUB, from the midst of the stones of fire. [17] YOUR HEART WAS LIFTED UP BECAUSE OF YOUR BEAUTY, YOU

CORRUPTED YOUR WISDOM BY REASON OF YOUR SPLENDOR. I cast you to the ground; I put you before kings, that they may see you."

From this passage of God's word, we are now to note three things for our present purpose about this same angelic being, of the order of angelic beings known as 'cherub.' The first is at verse 15, where God says, "You were blameless in your ways from the day you were created until unrighteousness was found in you." In other words, we see here that this angelic being, which God here calls a "cherub," was not only a created angelic being, but was also sinless from the day he had been created by God as part of His original creation until he sinned that first sin to occur in God's perfect sinless creation! Secondly, we are to see from verse 17 that God then says, "Your heart was lifted up because of your beauty; you corrupted your wisdom by reason of your splendor." In other words, we see again that this angelic being's heart was lifted due to PRIDE, which led to his sin. And then thirdly, we are to again see that God pronounces judgment on this angelic being, by letting us know that God will bring about his eventual downfall and bring him to an end!

What we are therefore to grasp here is that God is an eternal and uncreated Being, Who has no beginning or end; while human and angelic beings are simply created beings brought into existence by God to serve His purpose in time, with the end of human and angelic beings depending wholly on whether they serve God willingly or not during the time they have been allotted on earth! In other words, all have a choice, both human and angelic beings, to live in obedience to God or to rebel against Him and go one's own way. Both have eternal consequences! And now we see this angelic being, who was created sinless by God, now one day sin against God the original sin to enter God's perfect original sinless creation.

3) The entry of sin into the human race during the first age of time

We likely all heard the saying that 'misery loves company,' so that this created angelic being, who had now personally

47

sinned against God, as the first sin to occur in His perfect and sinless creation, now brings sin into the human race. And this event is also recorded for us in God's word, noting now what we read at Genesis 3:1-6, "[1] Now the SERPENT was more crafty than any beast of the field which the Lord God had made. And he said to THE WOMAN, "Indeed, has God said, 'You shall not eat from any tree of the garden'?" [2] The woman said to the serpent, "From the fruit of the trees of the garden we may eat; [3] but from the fruit of the tree which is in the middle of the garden, God has said, 'You shall not eat from it or touch it, or you will die.' " [4] The serpent said to the woman, "YOU SURELY WILL NOT DIE! [5] For God knows that in the day you eat from it YOUR EYES WILL BE OPENED, AND YOU WILL BE LIKE GOD, KNOWING GOOD AND EVIL." [6] When the woman saw that the tree was good for food, and that it was a delight to the eyes, and that the tree was desirable to make one wise, she took from its fruit and ate; and she gave also to her husband with her, and he ate."

There are a six very important truths that we now need to grasp for our present purpose from what we see taking place here. The first is at verse 1, where we see a certain character in the guise of a real serpent coming to the woman, who was Eve. And let us note what God later reveals to us in His word at Revelation 12:9 as to who that serpent really was here, "And the great dragon was thrown down, THE SERPENT OF OLD WHO IS CALLED THE DEVIL AND SATAN (Satan being the devil's name), WHO DECEIVES THE WHOLE WORLD; he was thrown down to the earth, and HIS ANGELS were thrown down with him." So we see from this verse that the serpent of Genesis 3:1 is really the devil, who is called Satan, which we are to grasp is the angelic being that we have just finished looking at in the previous section, as the one who sinned that original sin to enter God's perfect original creation. And now we further see here that he is the leader of other fallen angelic beings, which he also led into sin by also rebelling against God. And now these fallen angels, who are evil spirits, or demons, now serve the devil during time and for all eternity.

Then secondly, let us notice from verses 5 and 6 that the devil, who comes to Eve disguised as to what his true identity and intent were in order to deceive her, which he does with a lie, contradicting what God, Who is truth, had said to Adam at Genesis 2:16,17. And in this regard, let us note what God later says about the devil, first saying to unbelievers through His Son on earth at John 8:44, "YOU (unbelievers) ARE OF YOUR FATHER THE DEVIL, AND YOU WANT TO DO THE DESIRES OF YOUR FATHER. He was a murderer from the beginning, and does not stand in the truth because there is no truth in him. Whenever he speaks a lie, he speaks from his own nature, for HE IS A LIAR AND THE FATHER OF LIES," and secondly what God also reveals about the devil later at 2 Corinthians 11:13-15, "[13] For such men are false apostles, deceitful workers, disguising themselves as apostles of Christ. [14] No wonder, for EVEN SATAN DISGUISES HIMSELF AS AN ANGEL OF LIGHT. [15] Therefore it is not surprising if his servants also disguise themselves as servants of righteousness, whose end will be according to their deeds."

And so we see from these verses that the devil then is the originator of all lies, in the sense that he is behind all lies! Then it is important to grasp that all unbelievers have the devil as their "father," whether they realize it or not, and that all unbelievers seek to do the devil's will, knowingly or unknowingly! And we also see here that when the devil, or one of his fallen angels (as evils spirits, or demons), come to lead a human being into sin, it is never in a recognizable form. In other words, the devil does not let the person know that it is the devil in coming to them, as he always works by deception, which is a form of lying, by subverting the truth in such a way as to make the lie seem like the truth in order to accomplish one's agenda (will), which would not be accomplished if one were told the truth!

Then the third truth that we see from Genesis 3:1-6 is that the devil leads Eve into sin by lying to her and then promising something more than what she now has, in saying at verses 4 and 5, "[4] The serpent said to the woman, "You surely will not die! [5] For God knows that in the day you eat from it your eyes will be opened, and you will be like God, knowing good and evil." As a created being, the devil did not control death, God alone did. So what he said about death was a lie. Then in promising Eve knowledge that she did not have, namely the knowledge of good and evil, it appealed to her pride, something that the devil was already working on in coming to her in the first place instead of Adam.

What we need to see here is that Adam and Eve were yet innocent, meaning that they had never sinned. Up to now, all they knew about God, apart from each other and the physical world about them, was that God existed, and that He was The One Who had provided all that they had and saw. But they did not personally know God as a Person. This can be likened here to when a man chooses a wife, or a woman chooses a husband, they must first come to know each other personally by spending time together before they make the commitment of living their lives together. And that knowing each other was by means of knowing what the attributes that the other person had that one liked, with one eventually falling in love with the sum of that person. At this point, Adam and Eve were innocent, in terms of being sinless, but also in the sense of not personally knowing God. So the temptation of the devil to have this secret knowledge, "to be like God" and to "know good and evil," was a powerful temptation, which of course came with dire consequences for the human race, which will be felt right up the end of the ages of time and for all eternity to come!

And so, the fourth truth we are to see here is that both Eve and Adam partook of the forbidden tree of the knowledge of good and evil, thereby both committing a sin against God, with Eve's sin being that of pride; which not surprisingly is the same sin that the devil had sinned against God. So the first sin to enter God's original creation was through the devil, and was pride; and the first sin to enter God's human creation was through Eve, and was pride also! Adam's sin here was outright disobedience, since he disobeyed God's command to him at Genesis 2:16,17.

It is very important that we grasp that the knowledge of both good and evil would only come if Adam disobeyed God and sinned, by taking from the forbidden tree of the knowledge of good and evil. In other words, the knowledge of good, and its opposite evil, could only come through sin! And death could only come through sin also, as God had made clear to Adam at Genesis 2:17. And let us further note what God makes clear to one and all at Romans 5:12 of His word, "Therefore, just as through one man (Adam) sin entered into the world, and death through sin, and so death spread to all men, because all sinned." And what God means by "all sinned" here is that when Adam sinned against God by taking of the forbidden tree with Eve, he incurred a SINFUL NATURE, which means that from that moment onward, all that would come out of that sinful nature, as he lived by it – in thoughts, actions, and words – would be sin in God's sight!

And then that sinful nature would be passed on from the male through the female to their offspring in childbirth, with that sinful nature being then activated for each person born into this world from that point on when one reached the age of accountability, which is the age known only to God when a young child first learns right from wrong, and chooses the wrong, thereby becoming a sinner by nature and by practice, as personally accountable to God for one's sin! This also means that from that point on one is in need of redemption, because now subject to death! And what it also means is if a child dies before the age of accountability, which is known only to God as to when that is for each child, then that child has not personally sinned against God, being still in the original innocence of Adam and Eve, and will be with God in Heaven eternally at physical death!

And so we are to see that the reason that the devil lied to Eve and then deceived her with supposedly secret knowledge is that he wanted Eve to sin, thereby coming into bondage to him through that sin, which further meant that the devil would now be having human subjects as part of his kingdom, which would be his forever if they were to die in that state! It is clear then that in Eve being in innocence, not knowing good or evil – as would also be true of Adam – they could not as yet

51

recognize the absolute Goodness of God as yet, or the absolute evilness of the devil either, since the knowledge of good and evil would only come through committing sin!

Then the fifth important truth that we are to note from what we see occurring here at Genesis 3:1-6, is THE THREEFOLD TEMPTATION that Eve experienced before she actually sinned by eating from the forbidden tree. In other words, temptations to sin are never sin; only when we give in to those temptations do they become sin! And so we need to grasp here that these temptations were due to her interaction with the serpent, which we have seen is Satan, the devil, based on what he had told her at verses 4 and 5. And so we see these three temptation from what we read in the first part of Genesis 3:6, "When the woman saw that the (forbidden) tree was good for food, and that it was a delight to the eyes, and that the tree was desirable to make one wise, she took from its fruit and ate..." In other words, these three temptations led her into sin, which we are to see were PRIDE, GREED, AND LUST, which we are to realize are the three main sins by which the devil keeps the whole of the human race (principally unbelievers) in bondage to him by during the four ages of time!

We especially know this from what God later reveals to believers at 1 John 2:15-17 in His word, "[15] Do not love the world nor the things in the world. If anyone loves the world, the love of the Father is not in him. [16] For all that is in the world, the lust of the flesh (sinful lust) and the lust of the eyes (greed) and the boastful pride of life (pride), is not from the Father, but is from the world. [17] The world is passing away, and also its lusts; but the one who does the will of God lives forever." And so, what is important for us to remember from the above, in terms of learning about the devil and his schemes, is that the same devil is at work today as back then! And so, we are to see that the sin of PRIDE has to do with POWER, in being in CONTROL; that the sin of GREED has to do with MONEY, and the accumulation of money, which is not by God-ordained ways, such as hard work, but rather through UNLAWFUL MEANS. Then lastly, we are to see that the LUST OF THE FLESH here involved SEXUAL

SIN. In other words, it is SEXUAL ACTS THAT ARE FORBIDDEN BY GOD in His word! This is very important for us to keep in mind for when we look at the Deep State later!

Then the sixth truth that we are to see here is also from Genesis 3:6, where we see that in Adam and Eve having both now sinned against God, they are now seen to have sided with the devil against God, which meant that since they had been given the rule over the earth and all that is in it by God, that THEY WERE NOW WILLINGLY TURNING THAT GOD-GIVEN RULE OVER TO SATAN! Later in history, when God's Son did come to earth and was facing the same threefold temptations to sin at the hands of the devil at Luke 4:1-13, we see the devil make a very interesting statement to God's Son at verses 4:5-7, that we must now note, "And he (the devil) led Him (God's Son) up and showed Him all the kingdoms of the world in a moment of time. [6] And the devil said to Him, "I will give You all this domain and its glory; FOR IT HAS BEEN HANDED OVER TO ME, and I give it to whomever I wish. [7] Therefore if You worship before me, it shall all be Yours."

So it is very important that we see here that what the devil had handed over to him, which was not by God, but rather by Adam and Eve when they sinned against God, was the rule over this earth! That is why God later says in His word at 1 John 5:19, "We know that we (believers) are of God, and that the whole world lies in the power of the evil one." For what we also need to grasp here is that Adam and Eve were representative of the whole human race when they sinned against God in that garden of Eden, meaning that if any other man or woman had been in their place, they would have done exactly the same as what they did! Therefore, what they did in willingly turning the rule of this present world over to the devil was done on behalf of the whole human race, for we were all yet in the loins of Adam and Eve when they did so!

4) God making known that He will be sending His Son to earth as born of a woman, and that there will only be two seeds, or lines of descent, of mankind on earth during the four ages of time

What we then need to see relating to our present subject is that as soon as Adam and Eve had sinned against God, He makes known three very important truths at Genesis 3:15, saying this to the devil in the hearing of Adam and Eve, "And I (God) will put enmity between you (the devil) and the woman, and between YOUR SEED AND HER SEED; HE SHALL BRUISE YOU (the devil) ON YOUR HEAD, and you shall bruise HIM on the heel."

And so, the three truths that we need to observe, relating to what God just made known at Genesis 3:15 above, are: 1) That during time there will be two human seeds on earth, or two lines of descent, these being unbelievers and believers, who will always be in opposition to one another, because one is from the devil and the other is from God; 2) that God will send His Son to earth one day in the future, as born of a woman, in the same way that all human beings enter this world; and 3) that when God's Son comes, He will put an end to the devil and his works!

This last statement here we see in the last part of the verse, when God says, "…He (God's coming Son) shall bruise you (the devil) on the head, and you shall bruise Him (God's Son) on the heel." It is obvious that by a bruise on the heel God did not indicate what was a permanent blow. However, in saying a bruise to the head of the devil, God did indicate what was a permanent blow here!

So what God is doing in promising to send His Son to earth as born of a woman in the future is to introduce mankind to the gospel, that is, the good news relating to God's Son, as to what He will be accomplishing on behalf of mankind when He comes to earth, which God reveals for us later at 1 John 3:5,7,8, where God also makes clear there again that there are only two seeds on earth during time, there reading, "[5] You know that He (God's Son) appeared in order to take away sins; and in Him there is no sin… [7] Little children, make sure no one deceives you; the one who practices righteousness is righteous (and of God), just as He is righteous; [8] the one who practices sin (as a way of life, being an unbeliever) is OF THE DEVIL; for the devil has sinned from the beginning. THE SON OF GOD APPEARED FOR THIS PURPOSE, TO DESTROY THE WORKS OF THE DEVIL."

And what are the works of the devil? As we have seen, it was to bring sin into the human race, and through sin, death! What this means then is that for God's Son to destroy the works of the devil, He would have to first of all deal with mankind's sin! And this He did when He, The eternally existing Son of God, took on a human body prepared for Him in the womb of a virgin woman (noting Matthew 1:18-25 with Hebrews 10:5), Who was then born into this world and lived a sinless life for thirty-three and half years before being given into the hands of sinful men, who put Him to death on the cross, where God's Son died the death He did not deserve to die, in the place of a sinful human race which deserved to die (noting Romans 6:23 in part, "The wages of sin is death," in other words, death is the penalty due sin), that God might have a basis for forgiving the sins of any guilty sinner who believes that the death of God's Son was due one's own sins!

But then we need to realize that the death of God's Son in the place of sinners would deal with the question of sin, but then there remained the question of death. So then we see that the further good news that God makes known regarding His Son is that He not only died in the place of a sinful human race, but that He was also buried (as a picture of putting those sins away from God's sight forever), with God His Father then raising Him from the dead the third day, to then be alive forevermore to grant eternal life – the same righteous life that God ever has and lives, and which His Son also had and lived while on earth – to all those who would subsequently believe in God's Son to personally receive that forgiveness of sins and eternal life with God, which comes with a promise to one day be with God after this life. In other words, because God's Son was raised from the dead in order to deal with death, then that is how God deals with death, in that He raises from the dead all those who die during time; with those who believed in God's Son before physical death going to be with Him in Heaven, and those who remained in unbelief until physical death remaining with the devil, which is in hell, as where the devil will eventually have the throne and the subjects that he has been craving for since the moment he first sinned against God!

And so we see that at Genesis 3:15, God introduces us to some far-reaching truth! The one being that there are only two seeds, or lines of descent, of mankind on earth in time: The one belonging to God, which is the believers of the four ages of time, and the other belonging to the devil, which are the unbelievers of the four ages of time! Then the other important truth being that God would send His Son to earth one day to undo the works of the devil, which are sin and death, which God's Son does through His death for the sins of mankind, His burial to put those sins away from God's sight forever, before being raised from the dead the third day by His Father, for it is through His Son, as alive forevermore, that God imparts His life for one to live by to all those who during their stay on earth come to believe in Him! And so we see at Genesis 3:15 the gospel (God's good news relating to His Son) in a nutshell!

But before going further, we need to note that God gave Adam and Eve, who were now sinners in His sight, the knowledge of salvation, that is, of how a guilty sinner could be right with a Holy and a Righteous God, by giving them a practical display, noting now what we are further told at Genesis 3:7,21 of what happened immediately after Adam and Eve had sinned against God, "[7] Then the eyes of both of them were opened, and they knew that they were naked; and THEY SEWED FIG LEAVES TOGETHER AND MADE THEMSELVES LOIN COVERINGS... [21] THE LORD GOD MADE GARMENTS OF SKIN FOR ADAM AND HIS WIFE, AND CLOTHED THEM."

There are two very important truths to grasp from this. The first is at verse 7, which shows that Adam and Eve now tried to hide their shame of what they had done by making loin coverings for themselves, which is a representation of what sinful man has done ever since, which is to try to appease a Holy God by way of one's own works, which as we will see next is really the devil's counterfeit false religion! And then secondly, we are to see from verse 21 that what God then teaches them is that it is not through their own works that they can be right with God, but rather through the provision that God makes for them! So what we are to grasp here then is that in God taking the skins of an animal (which we know from later portions of God's word is a lamb, noting for instance John 1:29) to clothe Adam and Eve, God was letting them know that the innocent animal was sacrificed unto death so as to provide them the skins to be clothed with, with the innocent animal here foreshadowing God's eternal and sinless Son, Whom God had already promised at Genesis 3:15 that He would send in the future to undo the devil's works of sin and death!

What this further meant here then is that to be right with God in salvation a sinner must come to God and personally put one's faith in God's coming Son for the forgiveness of one's sins in order to receive eternal life from Him! In other words, man is not right with God through one's own works of righteousness, which the fig leaves Adam and Eve had made represented, but rather through the righteousness of God provided through faith in His own Son, which the innocent animal, from which the skins were taken, here represented. And now with this knowledge and in being clothed with God's righteousness, Adam and Eve were to pass on to their family and others the knowledge of God that they had gained, and especially of how a sinner deserving death could be right with a Holy God, which was through faith in His Son for the forgiveness of sins and the receiving of eternal life with God!

It would be instructive to see that God later teaches this same truth through the interaction of Abraham and his son Isaac at Genesis 22, where we see God tell Abraham to go and worship Him on a certain mountain with his son, Isaac. And when they get there, Isaac asks his father a question at verse 7, with the answer that Abraham gives him at verse 8, which we now need to carefully note, is a further amplification of the truth of Genesis 3:15 and 3:21, "[7] Isaac spoke to Abraham his father and said, "My father!" And he said, "Here I am, my son." And he said, "Behold, the fire and the wood, BUT WHERE IS THE LAMB FOR THE BURNT OFFERING?" [8] Abraham said, "GOD WILL PROVIDE FOR HIMSELF THE LAMB FOR THE BURNT OFFERING, my son." So the two of them walked on together."

And of course God did provide, with that lamb being a foreshadowing of His coming Son from Heaven to earth. So we are to remember that BEFORE God's Son actually came to earth as born of a virgin woman in the innocence of Adam, humans would place their faith in God's coming Son as foreshadowed in the animal sacrifices and offerings for the forgiveness of their sins and for the receiving of eternal life with God; and then AFTER God's Son actually came from Heaven to earth, humans place their faith in God's Son Who has already come, for the forgiveness of sins and eternal life, as it is today!

5) Seeing the devil establish a false religious system on earth

We need to keep in mind that from the beginning of his fall into sin, the devil's stated aim has been "to be like God," not only being equal to Him in terms of the height from which He dwells above creation, but also to rival Him in terms of establishing a counterfeit to all that he sees God do! And part of his plan since the beginning has been to have the human beings of earth in allegiance to him and to serve him, instead of God. This we have seen the devil do by leading mankind into bondage to sin, and now we need to see that the devil attempts to pervert God's truth relating to knowledge of Himself and salvation by establishing a counterfeit system of religion, so as to lead people away from God by never coming to know Him, and so remain in allegiance to him!

We know that the devil did institute such a false religious system due to what God tells us at Genesis 4, which was immediately after Cain and Abel had been born to Adam and Eve, who we must remember were now believers, with the knowledge of God and His salvation now resting with them in order to pass it on to the next generation. And so, let us now note what God tells us at Genesis 4:1-5,8 in part "[1] Now the man had relations with his wife Eve, and she conceived and gave birth to CAIN, and she said, "I have gotten a manchild with the help of the Lord." [2] Again, she gave birth to his brother ABEL. And Abel was a keeper of flocks, but Cain was a tiller of the ground. [3] So it came about in the course of time that Cain brought an offering to the Lord of the fruit of the ground. [4] Abel, on his part also brought of the firstlings of his flock and of their fat portions. AND THE LORD HAD REGARD FOR ABEL AND FOR HIS OFFERING; [5] BUT FOR CAIN AND FOR HIS OFFERING HE HAD NO REGARD. So Cain became very angry and his countenance fell… [8] And it came about when they were in the field, that Cain rose up against Abel his brother and killed him."

And before commenting on this, let us ask two very pertinent questions here. The first question is: Why did God accept Abel's offering to Him, but did not accept Cain's offering? And then the second question is: Why did Cain kill his brother Abel? What is instructive here is to see that God Himself gives the answer to both questions later in His word, noting what we read at 1 John 3:11,12, "[11] For this is the message which you (as believers) have heard from the beginning (noting John 13:35), that we should love one another; [12] not as CAIN, WHO WAS OF THE EVIL ONE AND SLEW HIS BROTHER. And for what reason did he slay him? Because his deeds were evil, and his brother's were righteous."

So here we see that God says Cain killed Abel because he "was of the evil one" (noting again John 8:44). And let us also note here what God says of Cain and Abel at verse 12, "his deeds were evil, and his brother's were righteous." In other words, Cain was an unbeliever rendering service to the devil, while Abel was a believer rendering service to God. We need to remember here that Adam would have shared the knowledge of salvation with both his sons, which resulted in Abel placing his faith in God's coming Son, which was why he offered God a sacrifice of an innocent animal, which God did accept, because he was showing by this that he believed in God's coming Son; while Cain rejected God's message of salvation, which is why he did not bring to God an offering of an innocent animal in sacrifice, and why God did not accept his offering!

So what we are to grasp from this is that the devil just established a false religious system on earth through Cain, which meant that God's plan of salvation was rejected and instead A MAN-MADE RELIGION WAS ESTABLISHED, WHERE MAN IN UNBELIEF SOUGHT TO BE RIGHT WITH God THROUGH ONE'S OWN WORKS! In other words, man's way was to bypass God's plan and substitute one's own, which is to think that what man provides will be adequate and acceptable to God. And so, right up to our present day, all false religious systems of men on earth, which God did not institute, all have as their basis this false teaching that my good deeds or works will get me right with God, and then into Heaven one day, no matter what that 'Heaven' might be conceived to be. God warns mankind in unbelief in His word at Proverbs 14:12, "There is a way which seems right to a man, but its end is the way of death."

6) The devil leads mankind in an attempt to establish the first one world government in history

What we are now to see is that the devil not only leads mankind into sin against God, and then not only leads them into a false religious system so as to keep them in unbelief; but now the devil seeks to lead mankind into attempting to establish the first one world government in history, and all of this before the first age of time even ends! And so, after the worldwide flood, in which God put to death all the unbelievers of earth, He once again repopulated the earth through the believers which remained, that being Noah and his three sons, plus their wives. But once again, as time progresses and due to that sinful nature which infects all human beings from the age of accountability onwards, we see many among their descendants choosing the same false religion of the devil and so remain unbelievers by rejecting God's way of salvation. So just as the first age of time was coming to an end, all the unbelievers of earth were gathered together in one place under one leader in the first attempt in world history to establish a one world government, with all these unbelievers being of course, knowingly or unknowingly, really in service to the devil while still in the bondage of sin.

So let us begin by first seeing the rise of this one world leader, that being an unbeliever named "Nimrod," whom God tells us about at Genesis 10:8,10-12, where we read, "[8] Now Cush became the father of NIMROD, HE BECAME A MIGHTY ONE ON THE EARTH... [10] THE BEGINNING OF HIS KINGDOM WAS BABEL and Erech and Accad and Calneh, IN THE LAND OF SHINAR. [11] From that land he went forth into Assyria, and built Nineveh and Rehoboth-Ir and Calah, [12] and Resen between Nineveh and Calah; that is the great city." And here we see the mention of Nimrod as being "a mighty one on the earth" and also see that "the beginning of his kingdom was Babel," which is an indication that he was a leader among the unbelievers of earth. This will become clearer from what God further tells us at Genesis 11, where God amplifies for us what occurred starting at Babel under Nimrod.

So let us now note what God further reveals to us at Genesis 11:1-5,8,9 "[1] Now THE WHOLE EARTH (of unbelievers) used the same language and the same words. [2] It came about as THEY (in reference to the unbelievers of verse 1) journeyed east, that they found a plain in the land of Shinar and settled there. [3] THEY said to one another, "Come, let us make bricks and burn them thoroughly." And they used brick for stone, and they used tar for mortar. [4] THEY said, "COME, LET US BUILD FOR OURSELVES A CITY, AND A TOWER WHOSE TOP WILL REACH INTO HEAVEN, AND LET US MAKE FOR OURSELVES A NAME, otherwise we will be scattered abroad over the face of the whole earth." [5] The Lord came down to see the city and the tower which the sons of men had built... [8] So the Lord scattered them abroad from there over the face of the whole earth; and they stopped building the city. [9] Therefore its name was called BABEL, because there the Lord confused the language of the whole earth; AND FROM THERE THE LORD SCATTERED THEM (all the unbelievers) ABROAD OVER THE FACE OF THE WHOLE EARTH."

Here we clearly see that the unbelievers of earth were united in three objectives, with the first being to build a city; secondly, they wanted to build a tower that would reach into Heaven, as where God dwells; and thirdly, they wanted to make a name for themselves! And here also, we are to see that the building of the tower to reach Heaven was akin to what the devil envisioned for himself when he first sinned against God, as we have already noted. So it is no wonder that God later says to the unbelievers of this world at John 8:44a, "You are of your father the devil, and you want to do the desires of your father." And so it is not hard to see the same sin of pride in these unbelievers, not only to counterfeit what God was doing, but to also reach God's throne in Heaven, to make a name for themselves and also seek to make themselves more important than God.

And for our present purpose, let us also note that in these unbelievers seeking to build a tower that would reach into Heaven meant they were aware, even though being subservient to the devil in their unbelief knowingly or unknowingly, that there was a true God, Who lived in a place called "Heaven," which was up there above the earth somewhere, and in their pride they wanted to not only be like Him, but to actually rule over all of God's creation instead of God!

And the import of the information given to us here is that this Babel in later history became the city of Babylon, which today is in ruins, being located within present day Iraq. And the additional import here is the fact that this city was the seat for centuries to come of the man-made false religious system on earth derived from the devil, which is why God, Who knows all things, later uses this fact to refer to this false religious system as just "Babylon," or "Babylon the great," in the book of Revelation. And the further import of what takes place here is that in God now scattering these unbelievers "over the face of the whole earth" this false religious system introduced into mankind by the devil is now seen as being spread into all nations on earth that subsequently arises! This fact now leads us to see what God does next to counter this.

7) God sets out to establish a believing nation, that being the nation of Israel, which would serve Him willingly out of love for Him!

What we are to now see is that starting at Genesis 12, which begins the second age of the time, we see God begin to do a new thing on the earth. We saw that as the first age of time ended God had desired to have believing nations on the earth, consisting of believers, who would spread the knowledge of God and of His plan of salvation to others, but which resulted instead in the earth having nations consisting of unbelievers in rebellion against God, under the rulership of Satan, the devil; all spreading a man-made, devil inspired, false religious system on earth!

And so, instead of ruling over His creation through Adam and his believing descendants, as God did during the first age of time, God now chooses one believer, Abraham, and through him, He makes a nation, that being the nation of Israel, with God then ruling over His creation through the believers of that one nation. So just as Adam was representative of all human beings in the first age of time, now this one nation will also be representative of all the nations of the earth during the second age of time, with God knowing that whatever this one nation did, any other nation would likewise do, if that nation had been chosen instead as a representative nation. In other words, God knows that the soul of mankind has been totally corrupted by the sinful human nature that all human beings have all over the earth, since all humans are descended from Adam and Eve, the first parents of the whole of the human race, who incurred that sinful nature, which has been passed on from male to female and then to one's offsprings at conception ever since.

And let us note that God had three reasons for establishing one nation, namely Israel, at this point in world history. The first reason has already been mentioned above, which was to have a nation of believers on earth, and through that one nation, to spread the knowledge of God, and especially the knowledge of how to have a personal relationship with God through faith in His Son, to all the other nations of the earth.

Then the second reason for God establishing the nation of Israel was to give His written word to mankind through the believers of this one nation. During the first age of time, man had been passing on the knowledge of God orally, and now for the first time in history, we have God's word being transmitted in written form through the believers of the nation of Israel. Then the third reason for God establishing the nation of Israel was due to the fact that God now desired to bring His Son to earth through the nation of Israel, to fulfill His promise that we have seen Him make at Genesis 3:15, where God said that His Son would one day come to earth, as born of a woman, to deal with the works of the devil.

8) God makes known that there will be five world-encompassing kingdoms on earth during the four ages of time, with four being of mankind in unbelief and the fifth being of God

What we are now to be aware of for our present purpose is that God prophesied through His prophet Daniel during the second age of time that there would be four kingdoms of mankind in unbelief that will be worldwide in scope during time, followed by one final kingdom, which will be of God. And so, beginning at Daniel chapter 2, we see God give this prophecy by means of a statue, with the constituent parts of the statue being to reveal the four world-encompassing kingdoms of mankind in unbelief. In other words, what Nimrod attempted to do in the first age of time, in terms of establishing a one world government, that is, a global government, God will now allow mankind to fulfill through four successive world empires during the second age!

And so, as we go through the book of Daniel, we discover that those four kingdoms, or world-encompassing empires, are to be Babylon, Media-Persia, Greece, and Rome. Then at Daniel 2:44, God reveals His own Kingdom as coming after these and replacing them by saying, "In the days of those kings the God of heaven will set up a kingdom which will never be destroyed, and that kingdom will not be left for another people; it will crush and put an end to all these kingdoms (that is, the four kingdoms of mankind in unbelief), but it will itself endure forever."

9) God then makes known the length of time He has allotted the four kingdoms of mankind in unbelief to exist on earth

What we also need to note for our present purpose is that it is also in the book of Daniel that God prophesied how long the four worldwide kingdoms of mankind in unbelief would have on earth, doing so at Daniel 9:24-27, which we now need to note and spend a few moments examining, with some words capitalized for emphasis and some notes added in brackets as a help, "[24] SEVENTY WEEKS HAVE BEEN DECREED for your people and your holy city, to finish the transgression, to make an end of sin, to make atonement for iniquity, to bring in everlasting righteousness, to seal up vision and prophecy and to anoint the most holy place. [25] So you are to know and discern that FROM THE ISSUING OF A DECREE TO RESTORE AND REBUILD JERUSALEM UNTIL MESSIAH THE PRINCE THERE WILL BE SEVEN WEEKS AND SIXTY-TWO WEEKS (that is, 69 weeks) ; it will be built again, with plaza and moat, even in times of distress. [26] Then after the sixty-two weeks THE MESSIAH WILL BE CUT OFF AND HAVE NOTHING, and the people of THE PRINCE WHO IS TO COME (who is the antichrist) will destroy the city and the sanctuary. And its end will come with a flood; even to the end there will be war; desolations are determined. [27] And he (that is, the prince who is to come, the antichrist)) will make a firm covenant.with the many for one week (seven years), but in the middle of the week he will put a stop to sacrifice and grain offering; and on the wing of abominations will come one (God's Son) who makes desolate, even until a complete destruction, one that is decreed, is poured out on the one (the prince who is to come, the antichrist) who makes desolate."

We cannot look in detail at this prophecy here only noting the relevant portions for our present purpose in this book. (If there are any readers who would like to read more about this, or the five worldwide kingdoms to come on earth during time, please see the author's book, "God's Prophetic Word To Mankind Through Daniel.") So let us then note the following seven truths that we now need to be aware of relating to this prophecy here at Daniel 9. The first is at verse 24, where God says that seventy weeks have been decreed by God for the nation of Israel during the second age of time, which we are to see refers not to literal weeks, but rather that each week refers to seven years, so that what has been decreed by God to occur here is in the span of 70 times 7 years, which is 490 years.

Then secondly, let us note from verse 25 that God does not begin the 490 years from the time of Abraham, as when He began to bring the nation of Israel into being, but rather God begins the 490 years "from the issuing of a decree to restore and rebuild Jerusalem...," which was after the city of Jerusalem and the temple of God there had been burned to the ground by the Babylonians, which destruction occurred in 486 BC. And thirdly, we are to see that God also gives at verse 25, not the end point of the 70 weeks, or 490 years of the prophecy, but rather tells us that after sixty-nine weeks, or 483 years, from the issuing of the decree, God's Son, Who will have come to earth by that point, as born of a woman as promised by God at Genesis 3:15, will now be "cut off," in reference to His death at the cross in payment for the sins of mankind.

Then the fourth truth to grasp is that this means there is one week, or seven years, left of the prophecy of 70 weeks to run its course during the second age of time, which will not take place until the present third age of time ends! But what happens at the time of the death of God's Son, The Lord Jesus Christ, is that three days later God's Son is raised from the dead by God His Father, then forty days later He ascends back to His Father's side in Heaven, with God then sending His Holy Spirit from Heaven to indwell the believers of earth to begin the present third age of time, as we see at Acts 2:1-4.

So what this means then is that when the second age was cut off after the 69th week of the prophecy, the Roman Empire was ruling the then known world from Rome. And so, the teaching of Christianity started on earth at a time when the then known world was pagan through and through. What this means then, and this is the fifth truth to keep in mind here, is that when the last week of seven years of the 70 week prophecy begins again, the same pagan (Godless) society that existed almost two thousand years ago will be prevalent as the present third age of time comes to an end, and of course, that is the case now, all over the world. What this further means is that this is one of the signs that this present third age of time is about to come to a close!

Then the sixth truth that we need to be aware of here is in the second part of verse 26, where God mentions "the prince who is to come," which we are to see is the coming antichrist, as the leader of a one world government on earth. And God says "who is to come," since he does not arise until the start of the last seven years left of the second age of time, which is the 70th week of Daniel's prophecy at Daniel 9:24-27, which is to be seen as "the one week" in view at verse 27. And of course, this last week of the prophecy does not begin until the present third age has finished running its course in the plan of God.

What this also means here, and this is a seventh truth to grasp and remember, is that the same Roman Empire that existed at the time the second age was interrupted, which was at the end of the 69th week of the prophecy, which is when God's Son, The Lord Jesus Christ, died at the cross, will now be the same Roman Empire that will be on earth, only at this point it can be called 'a revived Roman Empire,' being the nations of present day Europe, with the antichrist now arising out of one of these nations!

10) The devil's attempt to permanently do away with God's Son, which turns out to only be a bruise on the heel

What we need to do at this point is briefly show that once God's Son did come to earth – as born of a woman, as prophesied by God at Genesis 3:15 – that the devil did attempt to have God's Son, The Lord Jesus Christ, killed, at every opportunity that he had, doing so through the unbelievers of the nation of Israel, noting for instance what we read at Luke 4:28-30, "[28] And all the people in the synagogue were filled with rage as they heard these things; [29] and they got up and drove Him out of the city, and led Him to the brow of the hill on which their city had been built, in order to throw Him down the cliff. [30] But passing through their midst, He went His way."

As we see here, God The Father would not allow this to happen, since this was not the way appointed by God for His Son to die in payment of the sins of the human race, noting what God had prophesied, first, through His servant David at Psalm 22:14-18, as what His Son would later be saying as He hung on the cross dying, "[14] I am poured out like water, and all my bones are out of joint; my heart is like wax; it is melted within me. [15] My strength is dried up like a potsherd, and my tongue cleaves to my jaws; and You lay me in the dust of death. [16] For dogs have surrounded me; a band of evildoers has encompassed me; they pierced my hands and my feet. [17] I can count all my bones. They look, they stare at me; [18] they divide my garments among them, and for my clothing they cast lots," and then secondly as what God prophesied through His prophet Isaiah at Isaiah 53:5,6, "[5] But He was pierced through for our transgressions, He was crushed for our iniquities; the chastening for our well-being fell upon Him, and by His scourging we are healed. [6] All of us like sheep have gone astray, each of us has turned to his own way; but the Lord has caused the iniquity of us all to fall on Him."

However, the intervention of God The Father on behalf of His Son did not deter the devil from continuing to try to have The Lord Jesus Christ put to death by unbelievers, noting what we read next at John 8:20 and John 8:59, "[20] These words He spoke in the treasury, as He taught in the temple; and no one seized Him, because His hour had not yet come... [59] Therefore they picked up stones to throw at Him, but Jesus hid Himself (literally in the original Hebrew, 'was hidden') and went out of the temple." So we see that no man, even those unbelievers under the devil's sway, could touch God's Son, that is, until the time appointed by God had arrived for His Son to die, and that death being as God had prophesied, by having his hands and feet pierced through a crucifixion at the cross.

But when that moment had arrived for God's Son to die at the cross, then nothing or no one could stop it from happening. And so, when the three and a half year ministry of God's Son on earth was coming to a close; that is, as that 69th week of God's prophecy through Daniel was about to culminate with His death at the cross, the devil himself indwelt Judas Iscariot, who was the only unbeliever (noting John 6:70,71) among the twelve apostles who were with God's Son, as is clear from what God tells us in His word, first at Luke 22:2-4, "[2] The chief priests and the scribes (that is, the leadership of the nation of Israel in unbelief) were seeking how they might put Him to death; for they were afraid of the people. [3] And Satan entered into Judas who was called Iscariot, belonging to the number of the twelve. [4] And he went away and discussed with the chief priests and officers how he might betray Him to them," and secondly at John 13:27, which was when Judas actually leaves God's Son and the twelve and goes to the leadership to let them know that the time had now arrived for them to arrest God's Son, "After the morsel, Satan then entered into him (that is, Judas Iscariot). Therefore Jesus said to him, "What you do, do quickly." "

Then later that same evening, after God's Son had been arrested by those sent of the leadership of the nation of Israel, He said to the unbelieving leadership what we now read at Luke 22:52,53, "[52] Then Jesus said to the chief priests and officers of the temple and elders who had come against Him, "Have you come out with swords and clubs as you would against a robber? [53] While I was with you daily in the temple, you did not lay hands on Me; BUT THIS HOUR AND POWER OF DARKNESS ARE YOURS." And what God's Son meant by what has been capitalized here is that His time to be given into the hands of unbelievers in order to be crucified and die had now come, with the "power of darkness" here being in reference to the fact that from a human perspective, this was all a work of the devil, working through these unbeliever here, who were simply carrying out the devil's work!

However, from God's standpoint, it was a work that God was doing, in terms of using the sinful acts of the devil and of men in unbelief in order to accomplish His will on earth, as is clear from what God tells us Acts 2:22-24, with added notes as a help, "[22] Men of Israel, listen to these words: Jesus the Nazarene, a man attested to you by God with miracles and wonders and signs which God performed through Him in your midst, just as you yourselves know – [23] this Man, DELIVERED OVER BY THE PREDETERMINED PLAN AND FOREKNOWLEDGE OF GOD, you nailed to a cross by the hands of godless men and put Him to death. [24] BUT GOD REAISED HIM UP AGAIN, PUTTING AN END TO THE AGONY OF DEATH, SINCE IT WAS IMPOSSIBLE FOR HIM TO BE HELD IN ITS POWER," since that was God's Son in human flesh, and it is impossible for God's Son to remain in death. And so, we see here that whereas the devil thought he had the victory over God's Son, yet from God's perspective, it now meant that God's Son had here dealt with the works of the devil through His death and subsequent resurrection from the dead!

11) God making known the course of this present third age of time

Then we need to see what God makes known as to what takes place during the course of the present third age of time, as that which occurs from its beginning, when The Holy Spirit came from Heaven to indwell the believers, as we see at Acts 2:1-4; until its end, when God removes The Holy Spirit from the earth, along with every believer, dead or alive, as we see at 1 Thessalonians 4:14-17 with 2 Thessalonians 2:1-7. And so let us begin with what God tells us in a parable that He gives in His word at Luke 13:20,21, relating to the Kingdom of God (which is to be seen as God's rule through His Son in Heaven being outworked by all the believers of earth in the power of The Holy Spirit indwelling each), "[20] And again He said, "To what shall I compare the kingdom of God? [21] It is like leaven, which a woman took and hid in three pecks of flour until it was all leavened."

Here we are to see that the "leaven" represents, in general, the presence of sin (noting Luke 12:1 and 1 Corinthians 5:6-8), and FALSE TEACHING in particular, as is clear from what God tells us from the use of this same word at Matthew 16:11,12, "[11]"How is it that you do not understand that I did not speak to you concerning bread? But beware of the LEAVEN of the Pharisees and Sadducees." [12] Then they understood that He did not say to beware of the leaven of bread, but of THE TEACHING of the Pharisees and Sadducees," who were unbelievers here. And so we should not be surprised to see that throughout the present third age of time, from its beginning to its end, false teaching will permeate this world, which is the "flour" in view in the parable above at Luke 13:21. We must not forget that the originator of that false teaching is Satan, the devil himself, who started introducing lies into the truth of God, as we have seen back at Genesis 3:1-6, when the devil first came to Eve in the guise of a serpent!

Another very important disclosure that God makes to us regarding the course of this present third age, from its beginning to its end, is at Revelation chapters 2 and 3 in God's word, where God takes seven local churches then in existence on earth to show us the course of this present third age, noting for instance what God told the apostle John at Revelation 1:11, "Write in a book what you see, and send it to the seven churches: to Ephesus and to Smyrna and to Pergamum and to Thyatira and to Sardis and to Philadelphia and to Laodicea."

And God's purpose in giving seven messages to these seven literal local churches is to give us a chronological outline of the course of the present third age of time, also known as 'the church age,' which began in 33 AD and is fast coming to a close. In other words, in each of the seven local churches in view here, starting with Ephesus and ending with Laodicea, we have elements in each which will characterize the full length of the present church age. What this means is that

God knew before it did happen just how the present age would develop, and so gives us this outline through these seven literal local churches.

What is also important to keep in mind here is that elements of what the beginning of the church age was like, as we see for instance in the message by God to the local church at Ephesus, will still be present at the end of the church age, as in our own day; and conversely, in the elements of what will be found at the end of the church age, as mentioned by God in His message to Laodicea, was already seen as present during John's day, around 90 AD, when the local church at Laodicea was still in existence. In other words, there are certain elements given us in the first and last of these letters to these seven churches which are seen to exist throughout the length of the present third age known as 'the church age.'

We will not be going through these seven local churches in detail here, but rather will pick one element in the first local church at Ephesus, and also one element from the last local church named, which is at Laodicea, to illustrate what the first error to infect God's church on earth was, which will then be seen to infect the believers on earth making up God's church from beginning to end. And so, at Revelation 2:4, God begins by saying what is wrong in the local church at Ephesus, "But I have this against you, that YOU HAVE LEFT YOUR FIRST LOVE."

And what God means by "first love" here is their love for THE WRITTEN WORD OF GOD, which by extension then meant that they were moving away from God's Son, as THE WORD MADE FLESH (noting John 1:1,14)! In other words, these believers had departed ("you have left") from living their lives by the word of God only, as now children of God on earth! So what God is describing here is something which began early in the present third age of time and will carry on until the end of the age, so that God could later write to the seventh local church at Laodicea what we read at Revelation 3:20, which represents the spiritual condition of believers as the present third age comes to an end, "Behold, I stand at the door and knock; if anyone hears My voice and opens the door, I will come in to him and will dine with him, and he with Me."

So here we have God's Son in view, The Lord Jesus Christ, as standing at the door of that local church and knocking, with the promise being "if anyone hears My voice and opens the door, I will come in to him and dine with him, and he with Me." But the sad reality is that in one having left one's first love, one now no longer "hears My voice," of The Son of God knocking at the door! In other words, believers at the end of the present third age will be characterized as being in general so far away from living by God's word that they no longer hear the voice of The Son of God and so no longer fellowship with Him at all.

So we see here that if the devil cannot kill God's Son, then he will do the next best thing from his evil perspective, which is to attempt to prevent people from coming to personally know God in salvation to begin with, noting what we read at 2 Corinthians 4:3,4, "[3] And even if our gospel is veiled, it is veiled to those who are perishing, [4] in whose case the god of this world (Satan, the devil) has blinded the minds of the unbelieving so that they might not see the light of the gospel of the glory of Christ, who is the image of God."

And if the devil fails at that and a person does come to personally know God in salvation, then the devil will do the next best thing from his evil perspective which is to prevent a believer from serving God while on earth, by living in obedience to God's word. Let us recall that we have seen that at the beginning of time it was God's desire to have subjects who would not only believe in His Son, but who would also be serving God out of love for Him by living in accordance with His word. So we see that throughout each age of time, and especially during our present third age of time, the devil is doing all he can to prevent believers from even reading the word of God and serving God by living in accordance with God's word!

And as we close this section dealing with the present third age of time, let us note two passages of God's word, where God describes WHAT UNBELIEVERS WILL BE LIKE

DURING THE COURSE OF THIS DEVIL-INFESTED PRESENT THIRD AGE, which is at Romans 1:25-32, "[25] For they (the unbelievers of this present age) exchanged the truth of God for a lie, and worshiped and served the creature (having Satan, the devil in view here) rather than the Creator, who is blessed forever. Amen. [26] For this reason God gave them over to degrading passions; for their women exchanged the natural function for that which is unnatural, [27] and in the same way also the men abandoned the natural function of the woman and burned in their desire toward one another, men with men committing indecent acts and receiving in their own persons the due penalty of their error. [28] And just as they did not see fit to acknowledge God any longer, God gave them over to a depraved mind, to do those things which are not proper, [29] being filled with all unrighteousness, wickedness, greed, evil; full of envy, murder, strife, deceit, malice; they are gossips, [30] slanderers, haters of God, insolent, arrogant, boastful, inventors of evil, disobedient to parents, [31] without understanding, untrustworthy, unloving, unmerciful; [32] and although they know the ordinance of God, that those who practice such things are worthy of death, they not only do the same, but also give hearty approval to those who practice them." Let us remember this well for when we look at the Deep State in the next chapter!

And the second passage which we need to note is at 2 Timothy 3:1-5, where God now describes specifically WHAT UNBELIEVERS WILL BE LIKE IN THE LAST DAYS OF THE PRESENT THIRD AGE, "[1] But realize this, that in the last days difficult times (which can also be rendered 'violent times') will come. [2] For men will be lovers of self, lovers of money, boastful, arrogant, revilers, disobedient to parents, ungrateful, unholy, [3] unloving, irreconcilable, malicious gossips, without self-control, brutal, haters of good, [4] treacherous, reckless, conceited, lovers of pleasure rather than lovers of God, [5] holding to a form of godliness, although they have denied its power; Avoid such men as these." And again, if this does not describe a devil infested world, I do not know what does! So let us also keep this in mind for when we look at the Deep State in the next chapter.

12) The rise of the antichrist over a one world government during the last seven years left of the second age of time

As already mentioned, as soon as this present third age ends, which could be at any moment, God begins the last seven years remaining of the second age of time, which we have seen to be the case from God's prophecy of the seventy weeks at Daniel 9:24-27. So what we will do now is give a brief glimpse of the course of this seven year period, which is sometimes referred to as 'the tribulation period,' based on God making reference to it such as at Matthew 24:9,21,29. We have seen from Daniel 9:26,27 that God already alluded to an antichrist as coming during the latter part of the fourth kingdom of mankind in unbelief on earth, which is while under Roman world domination, which we have said now has reference to present day Europe.

We are also to note that after the book of Daniel, God did point to an 'antichrist' as coming on the world scene from what He later made known at 1 John 2:18, "Children, it is the last hour; and just as you heard that antichrist is coming, even now many antichrists have appeared; from this we know that it is the last hour." Let us notice three important facts from what God tells us here, with the first being that there is a person known as "antichrist" that "is coming." Then secondly, let us notice that God says, "even now many antichrists have appeared." And what is very important to grasp from this is that God is saying that there are many people during this present third age of time who could be characterized as "antichrists" simply because they are not only displaying the same character traits that the antichrist himself will have when he comes on the world scene, but these people are actually, knowingly or unknowingly preparing this world for his coming! Then the third fact we need to grasp is that whenever this second truth is seen as being a reality in the world, then we are to know that "it is the last hour" of the present third age of time, and so we need to be prepared for it will soon be ending!

And one reason for looking at the antichrist here is not only because it is part of the devil's work on earth in time, but it is also to help believers have their eyes open to what is going on at the present time, for the simple reason that when the antichrist comes on the world scene, IT WILL BE TO A WORLD THAT IS ALREADY PREPARED FOR HIM! In other words, this world will have been prepared by the devil for unbelievers to not only accept the antichrist, but to also be willing to serve him as ruling over a one world government! What this means then, as was noted above from 1 John 2:18, is that the CHARACTER TRAITS the antichrist will have when he comes will very much be present among the unbelievers of this world as the present third age of time comes to a close!

So let us go on then and look at the course of this seven year rule of the antichrist during the last seven years remaining of the second age of time, which God gives us a picture of at Revelation 6:1 to Revelation 19:21 in His word. In other words, in this portion of God's word, we have a God-given outline of what transpires on earth during those seven years under the rule of the antichrist. But again, since we cannot look at this whole portion here, since it would be beyond the scope of this book, let us look only at Revelation 13, where God gives us microscopic view of that same seven period, and where we clearly see the rule of the antichrist, with also a display of the character traits that the antichrist will have.

Therefore, let us quote Revelation 13:1-18 in its entirety here, with some notes added in brackets as a help, before we then comment in brief on portions that pertain specifically to our present subject, "[1] And the dragon (who is Satan, the devil, noting Revelation 12:9) stood on the sand of the seashore. Then I saw a beast (the antichrist) coming up out of the sea (nations), having ten horns and seven heads, and on his horns were ten diadems, and on his heads were blasphemous names. [2] And the beast (as the antichrist) which I saw was like a leopard, and his feet were like those of a bear, and his mouth like the mouth of a lion. And the dragon (the devil) gave him his power and his throne and great authority. [3] I saw one of his heads as if it had been slain, and his fatal wound was healed. And the whole earth was amazed and followed after the beast (the antichrist); [4] they worshiped the dragon (the devil) because he gave his authority to the beast (the antichrist); and they worshiped the beast (the antichrist), saying, "Who is like the beast (the antichrist), and who is able to wage war with him?" [5] There was given to him a mouth speaking arrogant words and blasphemies, and authority to act for forty-two months (which is three and half years) was given to him. [6] And he opened his mouth in blasphemies against God, to blaspheme His name and His tabernacle, that is, those who dwell in heaven. [7] It was also given to him to make war with the saints (the believers whom God will have saved at the beginning of the seven years) and to overcome them, and authority over every tribe and people and tongue and nation was given to him (thereby seeing that it is a worldwide rule). [8] All who dwell on the earth will worship him, everyone whose name has not been written from the foundation of the world in the book of life of the Lamb who has been slain (which means ALL unbelievers will worship the antichrist, bar none). [9] If anyone has an ear, let him hear. [10] If anyone is destined for captivity, to captivity he goes; if anyone kills with the sword, with the sword he must be killed. Here is the perseverance and the faith of the saints (believers). [11] Then I saw another beast (the false prophet, noting Revelation 19:20) coming up out of the earth; and he had two horns like a lamb and he spoke as a dragon. [12] He exercises all the authority of the first beast (the antichrist) in his presence (in other words, while the antichrist is the political leader during those seven years, the false prophet will be the religious leader of the false world religion, that is devil-derived and inspired, and he will be focused in serving the antichrist during the last three and half years). And he makes the earth and those who dwell in it to worship the first beast (the antichrist), whose fatal wound was healed. [13] He (the false prophet) performs great signs, so that he even makes fire come down out of heaven to the earth in the presence of men. [14] And he deceives (just the unbelievers of) those who dwell on the earth because of the signs which it was given him to perform in the presence of the beast (the antichrist), telling (the unbelievers of) those who dwell on the earth to make an image to the beast (the antichrist) who had the wound of the sword and has come to life. [15] And it was given to him (the false prophet) to give breath to the image of the beast (the antichrist), so that the image of the beast would even speak and cause as many as do not worship the image of the beast to be killed. [16] And he (the false prophet) causes all, the small and the great, and the rich and the poor, and the free men and the slaves, to be given a mark on their right hand or on their forehead (which only the unbelievers will take), [17] and he provides that no one will be able to buy or to sell, except the one who has the mark, either the name of the beast (the antichrist) or the number of his name. [18] Here is wisdom. Let him who has understanding calculate the number of the beast (the antichrist), for the number is that of a man; and his number is six hundred and sixty-six" (666).

The first comment we need to make here is that we see three evil characters being introduced to us by God, that being the dragon at verse 13:1, who is the devil; then the first beast also at verse 13:1, who is the antichrist; and finally the second beast introduced at verse 13:11, who is the false prophet. And it is clear from the end of verse 13:2 that the antichrist is under the devil's direct power and authority and sits on the devil's throne visibly while on earth. In other words, the antichrist, as the political leader, is ruling over a one world government, which takes in all the nations of the earth, as is clear from the end of verse 13:7, doing so visibly on behalf of the devil, who is unseen. And then the false prophet, as the leader of the devil's false religious system of earth, assists the antichrist, which is during the last three and a half years, which is when he comes on the scene.

The import of what has just been mentioned is that this evil trio are not human beings per se, but rather fallen angels! In other words, we know that the devil is Satan, a cherub, which is an order of angelic beings. What this means here then is that the antichrist and the false prophet must also be seen as fallen angels, that is, as demons only having male human appearance designed to deceive mankind on earth. What we need to grasp here is that when angelic beings, who are spirit beings, which do not have a body, nor are they visible; when these enter the physical world, they always take on male human appearance, which we see throughout God's word as indeed being the case. And that this evil trio here is the devil and two demons can be further grasped from what God tells us at Revelation 16:13,14, "[13] And I saw coming out of the mouth of the dragon and out of the mouth of the beast and out of the mouth of the false prophet, three unclean spirits like frogs; [14] for they are spirits of demons, performing signs, which go out to the kings of the whole world, to gather them together for the war of the great day of God, the Almighty."

What is critical for us to grasp here then is that what Satan the devil is attempting to do, which is to COUNTERFEIT GOD THE FATHER, THE SON OF GOD, AND THE HOLY SPIRIT! What this means then is that just as God The Father is always unseen, so the devil is unseen; and just as God The Father always works and speaks through His Son, The Lord Jesus Christ, Who is always the visible expression of God; then so too with the devil here, he works and speaks through the antichrist, who is called "antichrist," not only because he is opposed to Christ, but also because he attempts to counterfeit Christ, which is why, for instance, we see the antichrist pictured as having suffered a fatal blow and returned to life again at Revelation 13:3,12,14, simply because God's Son died and rose again from the dead again! So now the antichrist attempts to deceive mankind by doing the same, which is possible because angelic being do not die, with only the human body they have ever dying. And then we are to see that just as The Holy Spirit is on the scene of earth to make God's Son known, so too do we see the false prophet do the same from the time he arises during the last three and a half years of the second age of time, in terms of focusing on the antichrist and seeking to make him known on earth!

And now, let us go on and note the EVIL CHARACTER TRAITS that the antichrist displays during this seven year period, with the import for our noting this being because these are the same traits that will be seen among the unbelievers of earth in the last days of the present third age of time! But we do not want to draw this picture here only from the above passage at Revelation 13, but want to also include what God specifically says regarding the antichrist at 2 Thessalonians 2, where we will look at verses 1 to 12 for context, and again include some comments in brackets as a help, "[1] Now we request you, brethren, with regard to the coming of our Lord Jesus Christ (the first phase of His second coming) and our gathering together to Him (being when the believers of the present third age, who have died or who are yet alive, are now seen to be taken from the earth, as we see at 1 Thessalonians 4:14-17), [2] that you not be quickly shaken from your composure or be disturbed either by a spirit or a message or a letter as if from us, to the effect that the day of the Lord has come (with this "day of The Lord" in this case being in reference to the seven year period during which the antichrist is on earth). [3] Let no one in any way deceive you, for it (the day of The Lord) will not come unless the apostasy comes first, and the man of lawlessness is revealed, the son of destruction (in reference to the antichrist in these two terms), [4] who opposes and exalts himself above every so-called god or object of worship, so that he takes his seat in the temple of God, displaying himself as being God. [5] Do you not remember that while I was still with you, I was telling you these things? [6] And you know what restrains him now, so that in his time he (the antichrist) will be revealed. [7] For the mystery of lawlessness is already at work (during this present third age of time); only he (in reference to The Holy Spirit indwelling believers on earth during the present age) who now restrains will do so until he is taken out of the way (when The Holy Spirit is removed from the earth by God, along with all the believers of this present third age, as we see at 1 Thessalonians 4:14-17, then the antichrist will be revealed here on earth, as is clear from the next verse). [8] Then that lawless one (the antichrist) will be revealed whom the Lord (God's Son) will slay with the breath of His mouth and bring to an end by the appearance of His coming (which is at the end of the seven year period, as we see at Revelation 19:11-21); [9] that is, the one (the antichrist) whose coming is in accord with the activity of

Satan, with all power and signs and false wonders, [10] and with all the deception of wickedness for those who perish, because they (the unbelievers of the present third age) did not receive the love of the truth so as to be saved. [11] For this reason God will send upon them (the unbelievers) a deluding influence so that they will believe what is false (because already totally conditioned to believe lies), [12] in order that they all may be judged who did not believe the truth, but took pleasure in wickedness."

And now that we have the above passage in view, plus Revelation 13, let us go on here to note the most prominent evil character traits of the antichrist, which we must remember will be apparent in the unbelievers as this present third age comes to an end. And the first character trait that we need to notice here is that the antichrist will not only display an open hatred of God and of believers, but will also put himself forth as God and will seek to destroy the unbelievers of earth. Then secondly, which follows from this, is the antichrist will openly, knowingly, and willingly be serving Satan, the devil. Thirdly, the antichrist will be, as "the man of lawlessness," in total disregard of the laws governing mankind on earth, which are generally derived from God's word; but will instead be a law unto himself!

Then fourthly, we are to see that the antichrist, as "the son of destruction," will have no regard at all for the sanctity of human life, so that he is willing to be violent and kill without restraint all who oppose! And a fifth evil character trait is to display nothing but deception and lies; with a sixth being that he shows no restraint whatsoever in blaspheming God and what pertains to Him; with a last one to note here being that he will gladly be taking his seat and rule over a one world government with total control of all those on earth, believers and unbelievers alike! So, as we see here, what awaits us in the days ahead in not a pretty picture, which is why believers in particular need to have their eyes wide open now, this being a subject we will go into greater detail into in the third section of the book.

13) The coming of God's Son from Heaven to earth again at the end of the seven years in order to put an end to the reign of the antichrist and that of the false prophet

What we now need to briefly note at this point is that at the end of the last seven years, which ends the second age of time, we have God's Son, The Lord Jesus Christ, return from Heaven to earth again, to put to death all the unbelievers of earth, bar none (noting Hebrews 9:27), including putting an end to the reign of terror of the antichrist and the false prophet. The one passage that we will be noting here, where God tells us about these events, is at Revelation 19:11-21, which will be without comments, except some brief notes in brackets as a help, "[11] And I saw heaven opened, and behold, a white horse, and He (God's Son, The Lord Jesus Christ) who sat on it is called Faithful and True, and in righteousness He judges and wages war. [12] His eyes are a flame of fire, and on His head are many diadems; and He has a name written on Him which no one knows except Himself. [13] He is clothed with a robe dipped in blood, and His name is called The Word of God. [14] And the armies which are in heaven (consisting of unfallen angels and resurrected believers), clothed in fine linen, white and clean, were following Him on white horses. [15] From His mouth comes a sharp sword, so that with it He may strike down the nations, and He will rule them with a rod of iron (during the fourth age of time); and He treads the wine press of the fierce wrath of God, the Almighty. [16] And on His robe and on His thigh He has a name written, "KING OF KINGS, AND LORD OF LORDS." [17] Then I saw an angel standing in the sun, and he cried out with a loud voice, saying to all the birds which fly in midheaven, "Come, assemble for the great supper of God, [18] so that you may eat the flesh of kings and the flesh of commanders and the flesh of mighty men and the flesh of horses and of those who sit on them and the flesh of all men, both free men and slaves, and small and great." [19] And I saw the beast (the antichrist) and the kings of the earth (in unbelief) and their armies assembled to make war against Him (God's Son) who sat on the horse and against His army. [20] And the beast (the antichrist, as the first beast of Revelation 13:1) was seized, and with him the false prophet (as the second beast of Revelation 13:11) who performed the signs in his presence, by which he deceived those who had received the mark of the beast and those who worshiped his image (that being all unbelievers of earth, bar none); these two (the antichrist and the false prophet) were thrown alive into the lake of fire which burns with brimstone (which is the pit burning with fire below this present earth, mentioned earlier). [21] And the rest (consisting of all unbelievers of earth, bar none, noting Hebrews 9:27 again) were killed with the sword which came from the mouth of Him (God's Son, The Lord Jesus Christ) who sat on the horse, and all the birds were filled with their flesh."

14) God brings Satan the devil to his end, which is also in the fire of hell, forever

We need to remember, as we bring this chapter to a close, that at the beginning, we quoted Genesis 3:15, where God promised to give the devil a fatal blow and put an eternal end to his activity in opposing God and believers. And so, in having just seen God's Son deal an eternal blow to the antichrist and false prophet, who are now in the pit burning with fire under this earth, we see God now set up His Kingdom of Heaven over the earth, with His Son as King during the fourth age of time, and now seen ruling from the city coming down from Heaven as pictured by God at Revelation 21:10 to Revelation 22:5. And what we are to see first of all here is that as this fourth age of time begins on earth, Satan the devil is placed by God in that pit below this earth, where he will remain as a prisoner for the duration of the fourth age of time, which is a thousand years.

That what has just been said is so can be seen from what God tells us at Revelation 20:1-3, which we will not comment on except to provide some notes in brackets as a help, "[1] Then I saw an angel coming down from heaven, holding the key of the abyss (which is the pit, as the lowest part of Hades below this earth; with the word 'Hades' being the Greek equivalent to the Hebrew 'Sheol' noted earlier) and a great chain in his hand. [2] And he laid hold of the dragon, the serpent of old, who is the devil and Satan, and bound him for a thousand years (which is the duration of the fourth age); [3] and he threw him into the abyss, and shut it and sealed it over him, so that he would not deceive the nations any longer, until the thousand years were completed; after these things (that is, at the end of the fourth age) he must be released for a short time."

And so, after the 1000 years has elapsed, which means the fourth age of time is coming to a close and the eternal state is about to begin, which God has in view at Revelation 21:1-4, we see the devil being released from his prison from the abyss (the pit below this earth) to lead the unbelievers of earth, who will have arisen during the fourth age of time, into one final battle against God. And before we look at that, we need to keep in mind that during the fourth age of time, God repopulates the earth during that 1000 years of the fourth age from just believers remaining on earth at its beginning, same as God did when He repopulated the earth with just Noah and his three sons, and their wives, after the worldwide flood, as we have noted earlier. But due to humans on earth having a sinful nature from the time of Adam and Eve's sin onward, then the same occurs during the fourth age as occurred with Cain and Abel, in that some believe the message of salvation and become children of God, while others do not, and so remain on earth as children of the devil, being yet unbelievers. This will then explain what God tells us happens next in world history.

And so, after the 1000 years of the fourth age, as we were saying above, the devil is now released from his prison and leads the unbelievers of earth into one final rebellion against God, which only fails, with God now bringing Satan the devil to his final end, which is now in the pit of hell forever and ever! So let us note Revelation 20:7-10, where God tells us of these events, again without further comment, except for notes in brackets as a help, "[7] When the thousand years (of the fourth age) are completed, Satan will be released from his prison (the abyss, also sometimes referred to as 'the pit'), [8] and will come out to deceive the nations which are in the four corners of the earth, Gog and Magog, to gather them (all the unbelievers of earth, who will have arisen during the fourth age of time) together for the war; the number of them is like the sand of the seashore. [9] And they came up on the broad plain of the earth and surrounded the camp of the saints (believers) and the beloved city (the one in view from Revelation 21:10 to 22:5), and fire came down from (God in) heaven and devoured them. [10] And the devil who deceived them was thrown into the lake of fire and brimstone, where the beast (antichrist) and the false prophet are also; and they will be tormented day and night forever and ever." So let us take comfort in the fact that one day the enemy of God, and of all believers of time, will one day be no more! Amen, amen, and amen!

"For such men are false apostles, deceitful workers, disguising themselves as apostles of Christ. No wonder, for even Satan disguises himself as an angel of light. Therefore it is not surprising if his servants also disguise themselves as servants of righteousness, whose end will be according to their deeds."

2 Corinthians 11:13-15

CHAPTER FOUR

The Deep State

Now that we have looked at the rise of Satan, the devil, and of his evil intentions, from the beginning of time to the end of time in the last chapter, we are now in a better position to understand what the Deep State is. And so in this chapter we will seek to expose the Deep State, starting with a Biblically-based definition, so that we might be aware what President Trump, Q, and the Q movement are up against.

1) Seeing and defining the Deep State from a Biblical perspective

As we begin, let us note three passages of God's word that we have already quoted in the last section, which will frame a picture as given by God of how the devil works and who he works through, so that believers might know what they face when they face the Deep State. And so let us note again what God says about the devil and his workers at 2 Corinthians 2:11-13, which is also the quote used preceding this chapter, "For such men are false apostles, deceitful workers, disguising themselves as apostles of Christ. No wonder, for even Satan disguises himself as an angel of light. Therefore it is not surprising if his servants also disguise themselves as servants of righteousness, whose end will be according to their deeds." Here we see that the devil and the unbelievers of earth, who are in service to him, knowingly or unknowingly, do not work out in the open, but rather come as disguised so as to deceive and in order that one might not readily know who one is really dealing with. The devil does this in order to deceive, snare, and keep people in bondage to him!

A second relevant passage of God's word is at Ephesians 6:12, where God tells believers very plainly the following truth, "For our struggle is not against flesh and blood, but against the rulers, against the powers, against the world forces of this darkness, against the spiritual forces of wickedness in the heavenly places." Here God makes us aware of the fact that the devil not only has human accomplices in his evil work during time, but also other fallen angels, which are demons, or evil spirits, which work along with the devil from the realm of the spiritual world beyond our present physical world.

God says here that we need to beware as believers into thinking that our battle is primarily a physical one, as against foes which we can see, for the devil is unseen, and the fallen angels who are all in authority to him also work as unseen behind the scene! And so, that is why believers need God's armor and protection, as the verses following this verse points out to us here; not only because God is aware of and sees these dark evil satanic and demonic forces, but also because He is The only One Who has the power to deal with them and keep us safe!

And then as to the last quotes from God's word that we need to be aware of in order to properly understand the Deep State is to first note what God says at 1 John 5:19, where we read, "We know that we (as believers) are of God, and that the whole world (in unbelief) lies in the power of the evil one." What is also critical to grasp here is that it is not only the unbelievers of this world who are in the grip of Satan, the devil, due to their unbelief; but also this present world system! In other words, as believers we need to grasp that since the present earth is under the dominion of the devil, due to Adam and Eve, who had that dominion, siding with the devil when they sinned against God, as we have seen earlier; then this means that ALL in this present world is being used to serve the devil. So that is why God tells believers at 1 John 2:15-17, "Do not love the world nor the things in the world. If anyone loves the world, the love of the Father is not in him. For all that is in the world, the lust of the flesh (sinful lust) and the lust of the eyes (greed) and the boastful pride of life (pride), is not from the Father, but is from the world. The world is passing away, and also its lusts; but the one who does the will of God lives forever."

What this means then is that the devil not only works through the unbelievers of this world, whether they know it or not, and not only does he have authority over all the demons in the spiritual world around us, but he also controls this world system, which consists of all that God has not instituted in His word, the Bible. And now that we know this, we should all be able to give a Biblical definition of what the Deep State is, which can be regarded as THE VISIBLE AND INVISIBLE MEANS THAT SATAN, THE DEVIL, USES SINCE THE TIME OF ADAM AND EVE TO ACCOMPLISH HIS PLANS DURING THE FOUR AGES OF TIME, WHICH ARE TO REPLACE GOD WITH HIMSELF AS GOD, WITH THE INTERNT OF SETTING UP HIS OWN WORLD KINGDOM THAT WOULD ENCOUMAPASS THE WHOLE OF CREATION, FOR BOTH TIME AND ETERNITY! So let us keep this in mind as we go on with this chapter and also in the rest of the book.

2) The Deep State is worldwide, not just in the United States, although the United States, under President Trump, is to be seen as the main obstacle standing in the way of the Deep State

One truth we also need to grasp is that the Deep State is worldwide in scope, in terms of all nations and people groups on earth being affected, and not just the United States. What this means then, in relation to the subject of this book, is that President Trump, Q, and the Q movement, even though centered in the United States, are the main forces for good working to take down the evil Deep State, or at least hold it in check; also keeping in mind that the reality is that ultimately God WILL allow this present third age to end and for a one world government to arise under the antichrist! But until that happens, the reason that President Trump, who is CEO of the United States, and the Q movement, which is mostly based in the US – although now extending worldwide – are central to holding back and dismantling the Deep State, is due to the fact that President Trump has all the information on hand, through his military, of who the players in the physical realm over the whole earth are, what their crimes are, and what their sources of funds are!

And what we also need to grasp here is that the United States, as a sovereign nation, is also the prime target of the Deep State for the simple reason that the US is the leader of the free world, both economically and militarily, so that with their wealth and military might there is no power of men on earth which can defeat them. At the same time, the Deep State knows that as long as there is a President in the White House who advocates national sovereignty over globalism, then the desire of the Deep State to set up a one world government, which paves the way for the devil to bring in the antichrist, will be opposed. So the United States is the main target, as it has the means economically and militarily to cut the financing for the Deep State and also the power to put all the Deep State players to death or in jail.

3) The devil's three main human puppets that he has operating for him in his Deep State on earth at the present time

What we now need to see, which is something that Q has made known to us, is that the devil has three key human groups in the Deep State on earth that he operates through in order to bring in a one world government, as preparation for his bringing his antichrist on the world scene. These three, which Q has called the three sides of a triangle controlling the seen and unseen present world system, are THE HOUSE OF SAUD, THE ROTHSCHILD FAMILY, AND GEORGE SOROS. Again, the only reason we know this is due to Q having made this publicly known through the Q posts, noting now Q post #133 from November 11, 2017:

The Puppet Masters 133
Q !ITPb.qbhqo 11 Nov 2017 - 9:29:35 PM

Hard to swallow.

Important to progress.

Who are the puppet masters?

House of Saud (6+++) - $4 Trillion+

Rothschild (6++) - $2 Trillion+

Soros (6+) - $1 Trillion+

Focus on above (3).

Public wealth disclosures – False.

Many governments of the world feed the 'Eye'.

Think slush funds (feeder).

Think war (feeder).

Think environmental pacts (feeder).

Triangle has (3) sides.

Eye of Providence.

Follow the bloodlines.

What is the keystone?

Does Satan exist?

Does the 'thought' of Satan exist?

Who worships Satan?

What is a cult?

Epstein island.

What is a temple?

What occurs in a temple?

Worship?

Why is the temple on top of a mountain?

How many levels might exist below?

What is the significance of the colors, design and symbol above the dome?

Why is this relevant?

Who are the puppet masters?

Have the puppet masters traveled to this island?

When? How often? Why?

 "Vladimir Putin: The New World Order Worships Satan"

Q

A look through this post reveals a tremendous amount of information about our world system, as to who is really in control, and who it is they are really serving. It is not our purpose here to decipher this Q post in minute detail, but instead, we will concentrate on three key points there mentioned. So first of all, Q tells us that there are three visible puppet masters that are presently in control of this world, which again are: 1) the house of Saud, which as we will see is the principal family of Saudi Arabia; then 2) there is the Rothschild family, which is principally based in Europe; and finally, there is George Soros, who is now principally based in the United States.

What Q then points out about these puppet masters is the amount of money they control, which is not in the billions, but rather in the trillions of dollars! What is very important to grasp here is that the numbers given are only what is publicly known of them personally having, which Q says is not accurate, nor does it include all what they control. And so that is why Q tells the Q movement to focus on these three, even then giving us their principal means of income generation, which are many. There are two sources of funds not mentioned here, but are elsewhere, which are drugs and human trafficking.

Then secondly, Q tells us that these three puppet masters are the three human sides of the triangle, or pyramid, of the Deep State that is presently controlling this world. What this means, as we will see in a moment, is that each of the three sides of the triangle need to be taken down in order to take down the Deep State. In other words, as long as one or two sides of the triangle still operate freely in the world then the Deep State can still carry out its evil without constraints. So what this further means is that the principal way for President Trump and Q to take down the Deep State is to remove all their sources of funding, which is what is presently being done.

And thirdly, let us note from the above Q post that Satan, the devil, is mentioned, with Q then ending the post with a quote from Putin, the President of Russia, who said, "The New World Order (which is the Deep State) Worships Satan," with the reason for Q giving this quote being because it is true, as has been shown over and over again in the Q posts, and through the innumerable number of videos which have sprung up exposing the dark side of the Deep State.

And before we go on to another section here, let us note that in Q post #134, which is right after Q identified the three puppet masters in Q post #133 quoted above, we have Q starting to give us the US military operations under President Trump's command now starting to take down each of the puppet masters, beginning with the House of Saud in Saudi Arabia, which began with a purge on November 4, 2017. So let us note what Q revealed in a public way in Q post #134 on November 11, 2017:

Saudi Arabia Events Extraordinary 134
Q !ITPb.qbhqo 11 Nov 2017 - 9:29:58 PM
Why were the events in SA extraordinary?
Who was arrested?
What will bank records provide?
List names, family history, investment/ownership stakes, and point-to-point contacts.
EX: Alwaleed HUMA BO Citigroup US Control
Why is this relevant?
House of Saud.
House of Saud US Control
Follow the money.
What power shift recently occurred?
Was a new King appointed?
Coincidence?
Dark to LIGHT.
Why is this relevant?
One side of the triangle removed (1st time in history).
Other sides falling.
+++
++
+
Q

Please note that in the above post, Q tells us that the first puppet master, representing a key side of the triangle had now been removed, meaning that the House of Saud was no longer under the control of the Deep State! And then immediately following this information drop, Q made known, through Q posts #135 to Q post #138 a listing of all the Rothschild owned and controlled banks, which happens to be ALL the central banks of every country on earth, including the Federal Reserve of the United States; except for five small ones, which do not have a central bank. Here is a link to a video, titled 'Who controls our money,' which focuses mainly on the US Federal Reserve, but which will still give us an idea of what happens in every other country having a central bank as well, with this information being sure to open the eyes of many: https://www.youtube.com/watch?v=mQUhJTxK5mA.

Then let us note Q posts #140 and #142, which were given by Q on November 11 and 12, 2017, doing so here without further comments, as most readers should be able to follow the gist of the information being given. And here we should point out that Q here refers to the earlier triangle as the 'pyramid:'

Families Combined (TRI) = NOW 140
Q !ITPb.qbhqo 11 Nov 2017 - 9:33:51 PM
Wealth (over generations) buys power.
Power (over generations) buys more wealth/control.
More wealth/control buys countries and its people.
Families combined (TRI) = NWO.
Inner TRI families will collapse.
What is the keystone?
What Nation dominates all others?
What Nation has influence over most others?
What is the keystone?
Return to SA.
Strings cut (+++).
Puppets (+++) in shadows.
Each side of the triangle controls a certain subsect of power brokers.

Power brokers are also labeled as the puppets/servants.
What is the New World Order?
Why did POTUS receive a sword dance when visiting SA?
What does this mean culturally?
Why is this relevant?
What occurred in SA?
How did POTUS remove one side of the pyramid?
What did POTUS receive while visiting China?
Where did POTUS dine?
What is the significance?
What if China, Russia, and others are coordinating w/ POTUS to eliminate the NWO?
Who controls NK?
Who really controls NK?
Who controls several agencies within the US, EU, and abroad?
Why is No Such Agency so vital?
Enormous scale of events currently ongoing.
Why is Russia helping to kill ISIS?
This is not easy to accept nor believe.
Crumbs make bread.
Operations active.
Joint missions underway.
The world is fighting back.
Refer back to graphic.
The Great Awakening.
Snow White.
Iron Eagle.
Jason Bourne (2016)(Dream/CIA).
Q

Trace the Bloodlines 142
Q !ITPb.qbhqo 12 Nov 2017 - 10:16:24 AM
How did Soros replace family 'y'?
Who is family 'y'?
Trace the bloodlines of these (3) families.
What happened during WWII?

Was Hitler a puppet?

Who was his handler?

What was the purpose?

What was the real purpose of the war?

What age was GS?

What is the Soros family history?

What has occurred since the fall of N Germany?

Who is A. Merkel?

What is A. Merkel's family history?

Follow the bloodline.

Who died on the Titanic?

What year did the Titanic sink?

Why is this relevant?

What 'exactly' happened to the Titanic?

What 'class of people' were guaranteed a lifeboat?

Why did select 'individuals' not make it into the lifeboats?

Why is this relevant?

How do we know who was on the lifeboats (D or A)?

How were names and bodies recorded back then?

When were tickets purchased for her maiden voyage?

Who was 'specifically' invited?

Less than 10.

What is the FED?

What does the FED control?

Who controls the FED?

Who approved the formation of the FED?

Why did H-wood glorify Titanic as a tragic love story?

Who lived in the movie (what man)?

Why is this relevant?

Opposite is true.

What is brainwashing?

What is a PSYOP?

What happened to the Hindenburg?

What really happened to the Hindenburg?

Who died during the 'accident'?

Why is this relevant?

What are sheep?

Who controls the narrative?

The truth would put 99% of people in the hospital.

It must be controlled.

Snow White.

Iron Eagle.

Jason Bourne (CIA/Dream).

Q

It is highly recommended here that one read the first couple hundred posts by Q to get a sense of the global war being fought by President Trump and Q against the Deep State. One will be astounded at the sheer scope and depth of information being provided in the Q posts based on the military information being held by the Trump administration. This is not something that is being reported in the mainstream media, for the simple reason that they are not only part of the Deep State, but they are in fact being controlled lock, stock, and barrel by the puppet masters!

4) Deep State world bodies operating visibly on earth

We have just finished looking at the three puppet masters that the devil has operating on earth at the present time (the House of Saud, the Rothschilds, and George Soros), which he kept in bondage to himself through the three principal sins of pride, greed, and lust. As we have noted in the last chapter on Satan, the devil, the sin of PRIDE has to do with POWER, in one being in CONTROL; the sin of GREED has to do with MONEY, especially the accumulation of money, which is not by God-ordained ways, such as honest labor, but rather through UNLAWFUL MEANS. Then lastly, we are to see that the LUST OF THE FLESH here involves SEXUAL SIN. In other words, it is SEXUAL ACTS THAT ARE FORBIDDEN BY GOD in His word! And so these are to be seen as the three principal sins of the Deep State as given expression through all the devil's accomplices, having here in view human beings and institutions under his control in this physical realm. And so, in having looked briefly at the three puppet masters, let us now go on to note those institutions that are very much part of the Deep State and operate VISIBLY on a worldwide basis at present.

a) The United Nations (UN)

The United Nations (UN) was established on October 24, 1945, immediately after the end of World War II, and today comprises 193 nations of the world. It replaced the League of Nations, which operated between WW I and WW II. The UN's principal objectives are: 1) maintaining international peace and security, 2) protecting human rights, 3) delivering humanitarian aid, 4) promoting sustainable development and 5) upholding international law. The headquarters of the UN is in Manhattan, New York City, and sits on land that has been dedicated as its own city state, same as Vatican city within Rome in Italy. The organization is financed by assessed voluntary contributions from its member states.

Since the United Nations is the foremost visible institution being used by the Deep State to bring in a one world government means we should spend a few minutes examining its principal activities, which on the surface appear to be for the good of mankind, such as providing food to the poor, but are to be seen as being all part of the globalist agenda of bringing in a one world government! The scope of the UN, once it is fully known, will astound many. So let us begin by noting a United Nations system chart:

http://www.un.org/en/pdfs/18-00159e_un_system_chart_17x11_4c_en_web.pdf

And what would now prove useful is to focus for a moment on the principal arms of the United Nations that will show that IT IS ALREADY OPERATING IN THE CAPACITY OF A ONE WORLD GOVERNMENT!

World Health Organization (WHO)

The World Health Organization is the directing and coordinating authority on international health within the United Nations system. The objective of WHO is the attainment by all peoples of the highest possible level of health, which is defined as a state of complete physical, mental and social well-being.

World Bank

The World Bank operates in over 100 countries and is focused on poverty reduction and the improvement of living standards worldwide by providing low-interest loans, interest-free credit, and grants to developing countries for education, health, infrastructure, and communications, among other things.

World Trade Organization (WTO)

The World Trade Organization is a forum for governments to negotiate trade agreements, and a place where member governments try to sort out the trade problems they face with each other.

International Monetary Fund (IMF)

The International Monetary Fund fosters economic growth and employment by providing temporary financial assistance to countries to help ease balance of payments adjustment and technical assistance. The IMF currently has $28 billion in outstanding loans to 74 nations.

The International Maritime Organization (IMO)

The International Maritime Organization has created a worldwide comprehensive shipping regulatory framework, addressing safety and environmental concerns, legal matters, technical cooperation, security, and efficiency.

The International Telecommunication Union (ITU)

The International Telecommunication Union is the United Nations specialized agency for information and communication technologies. It is committed to connecting the entire world's people.

The International Labor Organization (ILO)

The International Labor Organization promotes international labor rights by formulating international standards on the freedom to associate, collective bargaining, the abolition of forced labor, and equality of opportunity and treatment.

The Universal Postal Union (UPU)

The Universal Postal Union is the primary forum for cooperation between postal sector players, helping to ensure a truly universal network of up-to-date products and services.

The World Intellectual Property Organization (WIPO)

The World Intellectual Property Organization protects intellectual property throughout the world through 23 international treaties.

The World Meteorological Organization (WMO)

The World Meteorological Organization facilitates the free international exchange of meteorological data and information and the furtherance of its use in aviation, shipping, security, and agriculture, among other things.

The United Nations Educational, Scientific and Cultural Organization (UNESCO)

The United Nations Educational, Scientific and Cultural Organization focuses on everything from teacher training to helping improve education worldwide. Its stated purpose is to contribute to peace and security by promoting international collaboration through educational, scientific, and cultural reforms in order to increase universal respect for justice, the rule of law, and human rights along with fundamental freedom proclaimed in the United Nations Charter.

As can be seen from the above PARTIAL LIST, the United Nations operates on a global scale and in every area of human life! But before we leave our look at the United Nations as the foremost visible vehicle being presently used by the Deep State globalists to bring in a one world government, we need to point out a very far reaching recent development at the United Nations, which was the GLOBAL COMPACT for MIGRATION (GCM), which was adopted by the UN general assembly on December 19, 2018. And what many are not aware of is that this compact MAKES MIGRATION A HUMAN RIGHT! And so, let us keep in mind as we continue that the United Nations is simply a tool of the Deep State toward the establishment of a one world government!

b) World Economic Forum (WEF)

Another world body that the Deep State uses to push its globalist agenda of bringing in a one world government, apart from the United Nations, is the World Economic Forum, based in Geneva, Switzerland, and founded in 1971. The Forum's mission is to improve the state of the world by engaging business, political, academic, and other leaders of society to shape global, regional, and industry agendas. The WEF hosts an annual meeting at the end of January in Davos, Switzerland, for the English speaking world, where some 2,500 business leaders, international political leaders, economists, celebrities and journalists gather for up to four days to discuss the most pressing issues facing the world.

The WEF further holds other non-English annual meetings, that being in China, India, and the United Arab Emirates, plus some six to eight regional meetings each year in locations across Africa, East Asia and Latin America. It also produces a series of research reports and engages its members in sector-specific initiatives. As is quite evident, the WEF seeks to especially provide a platform for leaders from all stakeholder groups from around the world – business, government and civil society – to come together.

c) Council on Foreign Relations (CFR)

Another influential Deep State instrument is the Council on Foreign Relations, which was founded in 1921 and is headquartered in New York City. It is a United States nonprofit think tank specializing in U.S. foreign policy and international affairs. Its membership, which numbers about

4,900, has included senior politicians, more than a dozen secretaries of state, CIA directors, bankers, lawyers, professors, and senior media figures.

The CFR meetings convene government officials, global business leaders and prominent members of the intelligence and foreign-policy community to discuss international issues. CFR publishes the bi-monthly journal Foreign Affairs, and runs the David Rockefeller Studies Program, which influences foreign policy by making recommendations to the presidential administration and diplomatic community, testifying before Congress, interacting with the media, and publishing on foreign policy issues.

d) The Trilateral Commission

Yet another influential Deep State instrument is the Trilateral Commission, which is a non-governmental, policy-oriented forum that was formed in 1973 by private citizens of Japan, North American nations (the U.S. and Canada), and Western European nations to foster substantive political and economic dialogue across the world. It brings together leaders in their individual capacity from the worlds of business, government, academia, press and media, as well as civil society. The Commission offers a global platform for open dialogue, reaching out to those with different views and engaging with decision makers from around the world with the aim of finding solutions to the great geopolitical, economic and social challenges of our time.

Its members are also committed to supporting a rules-based international system, closer cooperation across borders and respect for the diversity of approaches to policy issues. Here is a quote from its founding document, "Growing interdependence is a fact of life of the contemporary world. It transcends and influences national systems... While it is important to develop greater cooperation among all the countries of the world, Japan, Western Europe, and North America, in view of their great weight in the world economy and their massive relations with one another, bear a special responsibility for developing effective cooperation, both in their own interests and in those of the rest of the world."

e) European Union (EU)

Coming now to across the pond, we have the devil's second most important vehicle, after the United Nations, for forming a one world government, which is the European Union, which is a political and economic union of 28 member states that cover much of present day Europe. It has a population of about 513 million and is the largest trading block in the world by GDP. The EU has developed an internal single market through a standardized system of laws that apply in all member states, which have agreed to act as one. EU policies aim to ensure the free movement of people, goods, services and capital within the European Union. A monetary union was established in 1999 and 19 nations of the European Union currently use the euro currency. What is important to keep in mind here is that according to God's word the antichrist will arise from one of the countries of present-day Europe!

f) Mainstream and social media

Since globalists know that it is impossible to have a one world government without also controlling what people read, see, or hear, then they have made sure that they are in control of the mainstream media, which consists of every form of media that might be out there by which people receive the news, pertaining to what is going on in the world. These would include such entities as CNN, ABC, CBS, NBC, MNBC, Google, YouTube, Facebook, Twitter, Instagram, New York Times, Washington Post, etc., any that are seen to censor Conservative thought or any relating to President Trump and his administration.

Therefore, the mainstream media is to be seen as an integral and necessary part of the Deep State, for these people know that if they control the narrative, then they control the views that people hold regarding people and events occurring worldwide, even if that information is knowingly false. However, one thing is sure, the Deep State will make ensure that the narrative put forth is in line with the ideology that they want people to hold!

g) Big Pharma

The term "Big Pharma" is being used here to identify an industry that developed in the United States in the early 1900's and has since spread worldwide, which has five main components that enables it to survive, these being the pharmaceutical companies, the doctors, the hospitals, the regulatory apparatus, and medical publications. And what is key to understanding Big Pharma is knowing that this industry is FOR PROFIT, which are derived from PATENTS of drugs or compounds that are MAN-MADE, that is, made in a laboratory.

What existed in the United States in the early 1900's was a system of health that had been a continuation of what had been practiced in Europe, especially, over the previous centuries, where the individual was treated by mostly natural means, with the underlying belief being that the body could heal itself if given the right conditions. This natural approach looked at the whole person, and especially one's diet, when seeking to help a person heal.

However, since anything that is found in nature cannot be patented, meant that one could not make any money off this system. And so in the early 1900's, the Carnegie Foundation commissioned a man named Abraham Flexner to visit all 155 medical schools then existing in the United States and Canada, resulting in the Flexner Report in 1910, which advocated for a medical system based on science, rather than what was then existing, with the model being advocated being that already in place at John Hopkins University School of Medicine in Baltimore, Maryland.

With this as background, one should now watch the following two videos, which have been carefully selected. The first one is titled, "Who made MD's king." It is a talk by a Naturopathic doctor and is very informative and revealing. And before one looks at the video, please be aware that this is part of a sales pitch for a network selling a brand of supplements. So, what I recommend here is just the first 45 minutes or so, where he shares the most valuable information that we should all be aware of regarding Big Pharma. So here is the video link, https://www.youtube.com/watch?v=blxeEHV1lio

Then the second very informative and revealing video, which may make one cry, especially if one has lost loved ones to cancer, is titled, "Cancer: The Forbidden Cures," and will give one a good idea of the two system's approach to health now in place, which today are dubbed by the medical establishment as 'modern medicine' and 'alternative medicine:'

https://www.youtube.com/watch?v=zmQZcj3Cggl

h) Word Government Summit

The World Government Summit is an annual event that has been held in Dubai, United Arab Emirates (UAE) since 2013, and now has about 150 countries participating. It is the only global organization dedicated to shaping the future of governments and setting the agenda for the next generation of governments worldwide. The Word Government Summit brings together leaders in government for a global dialogue about governmental process and policies with a focus on the issues of futurism, technology and innovation. The summit acts as a knowledge exchange hub between government officials, thought leaders, policy makers and private sector leaders.

i) Singularity University (SU)

Another recent development, along with the World Government Summit, is Singularity University, which is actually a corporation established in Silicon Valley, California, in 2009, that also has the goal of preparing global leaders and institutions for the future. Its mission is to empower individuals and organizations across the globe to learn, connect, and innovate breakthrough solutions using accelerating technologies like artificial intelligence, robotics, and digital biology. To achieve this, they offer educational programs, courses, and summits; enterprise strategy, leadership, and innovation programs. The Singularity University community includes entrepreneurs, corporations, global nonprofits, governments, and academic institutions in more than 127 countries.

j) World Council of Churches (WCC)

Then there is the World Council of Churches, which is a worldwide inter-church organization founded in 1948 and based at the Ecumenical Centre in Geneva, Switzerland. The WCC is a worldwide fellowship of 349 global, regional and sub-regional, national and local church groups, seeking unity, a common witness and Christian service. The organization's members include denominations which claim to collectively represent some 590 million people across the world in about 150 countries, including 520,000 local congregations served by 493,000 pastors and priests, elders, teachers, members of parish councils and others. And although the Catholic Church is not a member, it still sends accredited observers to meetings.

What is important to observe here is that in the previous chapter, when looking at Revelation 13, as when the antichrist will be on earth as political leader of a one world government over the nations of the earth, he will have as assistant the false prophet, who is the religious leader of the false religious system of the earth, which we there saw had been instituted by Satan, the devil, back at the time of Cain. And so, it is no coincidence to now see from this section that the globalist Deep State is seeking to move the nations of the world toward a unified mankind, along both political and religious lines, so that this world will then be ready for the introduction of the antichrist and the false prophet!

5) Deep State world bodies operating secretly on earth

Now that we have looked at some of the VISIBLE human institutions that the devil and the Deep State use in order to bring in a one world government, let us go on to look in this section at those human institutions, which although known by some, yet remain SECRETIVE as to the true nature of their operations. We will only deal with more current secret organizations here, which mean that there are many more, which date back centuries and these are still very much affecting our present world. Many of these will be encountered by any readers doing research on the Q posts in the coming days. And so, some of these secret institutions, organizations, or societies are:

Bilderberg Meeting

The Bilderberg Meeting, also unofficially called the "Bilderberg Group", "Bilderberg conference" or "Bilderberg Club," is an annual conference established in 1954 by Prince Bernhard of the Netherlands, which has the principal aim of fostering dialogue between Europe and North America. Participants are European and North American political leaders, experts from industry, finance, academia, and the media. The meetings are held under the Chatham House Rule, which states, "participants are free to use the information received, but neither the identity nor the affiliation of the speaker(s) nor of any other participant may be revealed," which is the main reason for it usually being designated as a secret society.

Freemasonry

Freemasonry is a secret fraternal (men-only) order of Free and Accepted Masons, the largest worldwide secret society. Spread by the advance of the British Empire, Freemasonry remains most popular in the British Isles and in other countries originally within the empire. Estimates of the worldwide membership of Freemasonry in the early 21st century ranged from about two million to more than six million.

Freemasonry evolved from the guilds of stonemasons and cathedral builders of the Middle Ages. With the decline of cathedral building, some lodges of masons began to accept honorary members to bolster their declining membership. From a few of these lodges developed modern symbolic or speculative Freemasonry, which particularly in the 17th and 18th centuries adopted the rites and trappings of ancient religious orders and of chivalric brotherhoods.

In addition to the main bodies of Freemasonry derived from the British tradition, there are also a number of appendant groups that are primarily social or recreational in character, having no official standing in Freemasonry but drawing their membership from the higher degrees of the society. They are especially prevalent in the United States and are among those known for their charitable work, such as the Ancient Arabic Order of the Nobles of the Mystic Shrine (the "Shriners"). In Britain and certain other countries there are separate lodges restricted to women.

Bohemian Grove

Bohemian Grove is an all-male secret society that is part of the Bohemian Club, which sits on a 2700 acre property in Monte Rio, California. It has been in operation since 1872 and is particularly famous due to its more than two week July encampment of men of power, like former President Reagan, Clinton, Herbert H Bush and George W Bush, including many prominent business leaders, government officials, and senior media executives. Because of the high positions of the attendees, the property is equipped with year round sophisticated security, including armed guards.

The main event of the summer gathering is 'The Cremation of Care' ceremony, which is a theatrical production in which some of the club's members participate as actors. The Cremation of Care was separated from the other Grove Plays in 1913 and moved to the first night and is said to have become "an exorcising of the demon to ensure the success of the ensuing two weeks." The ceremony takes place in front of the Owl Shrine. The moss and lichen-covered statue simulates a natural rock formation, yet holds electrical and audio equipment within it. One can get a good glimpse of the Bohemian Grove gathering and what goes on there from the video: https://www.youtube.com/watch?v=5UM3KbmfoG4

Skull and Bones

This secret society, founded in 1832 at Yale University in New Haven, Connecticut, is included here only because its members, who are all alumni of Yale, hold important positions in world affairs. For instance, Herbert H Bush, the 41st President of the United States, was a member before he died; as also his son, George W Bush, the 43rd President; and also John Kerry, former Presidential nominee for the Democratic Party and former Secretary of State under President Obama. Members, often referred to as 'Bonesmen,' meet in a building called 'the Tomb,' and also have a retreat on the St-Lawrence River called 'Deer Island.'

What would be useful at this point is give a link to a video presentation by Alex Newman, who is Foreign Correspondent for the New American magazine, which is a publication of the John Birch Society, which is an organization founded in 1958 by the Bible-believing Christian, Robert W Welch Jr, which has chapters nationwide. Here is the link to the video, which is titled, 'America under siege, the Deep State:' https://www.youtube.com/watch?v=6YUcUoFveJc. The value of this video is that it touches on some of the Deep State secret societies that we have just mentioned above.

Central Intelligence Agency (CIA)

What you will now read will not only blow your mind, as it did mine, but it will also make you think that I indeed am a conspiracy theorist, which of course I am not, nor have I ever been or ever plan in becoming. But the truth that has come out in the Q posts so far is that the CIA is, and has been, a tool of the Deep State for many years. Even though the CIA is located in Langley, Virginia, and has the stated mission of preempting threats and further US national security objectives by collecting intelligence that matters, producing objective all-source analysis, conducting effective covert action as directed by the President, and safeguarding the secrets that help keep the United States safe, nevertheless, this intelligence agency has nevertheless gone rogue, and does not at the moment serve the interests of the current President, but rather those of the Deep State!

The CIA was first created on July 26, 1947, when Harry S. Truman signed the National Security Act into law, with this being done largely as a result of the unforeseen attack on Pearl Harbor by Japan on December 7, 1941. .Unlike the

Federal Bureau of Investigation (FBI), which is a domestic security service, the CIA has no law enforcement function and is mainly focused on overseas intelligence gathering, as a civilian foreign intelligence service of the federal government of the United States, tasked with gathering, processing, and analyzing national security information from around the world. Before 2004, the CIA was the principal civilian intelligence agency of the federal government, but as a result of the September 11, 2001, terror attacks; the CIA is now organized under the Director of National Intelligence (DNI).

That the CIA is now seen as tool of the Deep State, in that it operates to serve the Deep State's objective of establishing a one world government, is based on information provided on the Q map global themes and also from a few of the Q posts. So first, let us note what has been made known about the CIA from the Q map global themes:

i) **Iran.** The Iran Nuke deal was a scam. It was never about nuclear disarmament or prevention. It was about lifting sanctions and opening a new untapped market for EU companies; it was about securing a black ops site for the **CIA**. This is why Obama sealed the Iran deal under a top secret classification and why Congress could not view it. Iran obtained uranium via the Uranium One scandal/exchange. Iran obtained billions in funding from the Obama admin (hard cash pallets + wire transfers). EU leaders were complicit in this scheme and received kickbacks/bribes. Iran will be FREED from NWO/CIA control just like North Korea has been FREED.

ii) **North Korea** (NK) was not run by Kim Jung-un. NK was a **CIA** black ops site. NK was used by the Cabal/NWO as leverage over other countries and for protection. The NK nuclear threat was real (NK had miniaturization tech in 2004 and ICBM tech in 2009). NK received uranium via the Uranium One scandal. NK received missile/nuke tech from Operation Merlin (Nasa/SpaceX/SAPs) and received funding as part of the Iran deal. NK was to be the war engine to ignite World War III. This was the biggest cover-up in our history and POTUS stopped it ALL. NK is now FREED from **CIA** control and on the path to peace!

iii) **MKUltra** is the code name given to a top secret **CIA** program of mind control experimentation on human subjects. These experiments were sometimes performed on the general population without consent (illegal). CIA informed Congress many years ago that the program was discontinued; however the opposite was true, and the program has evolved considerably. Here's how it works: 1) CIA selects individuals (pawns) with certain mental conditions/ susceptibilities. 2) CIA arranges for "therapy sessions" and the prescription of psychotropic drugs. 3) CIA breaks the mind into a functional/programmable device that can triggered by mobile phone signals. 4) These mind controlled pawns hear voices/demons in their heads that trigger/instruct them to commit horrible acts of violence (e.g., school shootings).

iv) **Las Vegas.** The 2017 Las Vegas shooting occurred on the night of Sunday, October 1, 2017 when a gunman opened fire on a crowd of concertgoers at the Route 91 Harvest music festival on the Las Vegas Strip in Nevada, leaving 58 people dead and 851 injured. Q has suggested that: 1) The shooter was a spook (**CIA** agent), a stooge selected for his background (white loner), forced to do the shooting (family held hostage), and then terminated (no evidence). 2) The "reported" gunfire came from the top floors of the Mandalay Bay Hotel, owned by Saudi Prince Al-Waleed. 3) MS-13 thugs were involved somehow and there was more than one shooter (like JFK assassination). 4) Survivors who were organizing on social media talking about multiple shooters have been systematically killed off. 5) POTUS was in Las Vegas that night (unmarked plane) for a classified meeting and was LIKELY the primary target (assassination attempt).

v) **The National Security Agency** (NSA) is responsible for global monitoring, collection, and processing of information and data for foreign intelligence and counterintelligence purposes. NSA has all the information, nothing is deleted, and is helping POTUS and Military Intelligence (MI) drain the swamp, that is, **purge the Deep State, and combat the Clowns in America (CIA).**

That the CIA is a tool of the Deep State and is operating as a covert operation of the Deep State, and no longer at the direction of the President, can be seen from two recent Q posts! First, let us note Q post #2988 from March 6th, 2019:

DARPA = FACEBOOK 2988
Q !!mG7VJxZNCl 6 Mar 2019 - 9:38:12 PM
https://twitter.com/amyboo69/status/1103512061693161472
■

Define 'Lifelog' [DARPA].

"an ontology-based (sub)system that captures, stores, and makes accessible the flow of one person's experience in and interactions with the world in order to support a broad spectrum of associates/assistants and other system capabilities". The objective of the LifeLog concept was "to be able to trace the 'threads' of an individual's life in terms of events, states, and relationships", and it has the ability to "take in all of a subject's experience, from phone numbers dialed and e-mail messages viewed to every breath taken, step made and place gone".

Define 'FB'.

The Facebook service can be accessed from devices with Internet connectivity, such as personal computers, tablets and smartphones. After registering, users can create a customized profile revealing information about themselves. Users can post text, photos and multimedia of their own devising and share it with other users as "friends". Users can use various embedded apps, and receive notifications of their friends' activities. Users may join common-interest groups.

Compare & Contrast.

DARPA senior employees > FB?

DARPA TERMINATES PROGRAM FEB 4, 2004.

FB FOUNDED FEB 4, 2004.

DARPA = FB

Q

Then secondly, let us note Q post #2989, also from March 6th, 2019:

Facebook is Owned & Operated by the CIA 2989

Q !!mG7VJxZNCI 6 Mar 2019 - 9:58:23 PM

Logical thinking.

Did DARPA complete build/code (tax-payer funded) 'LifeLog' program?

After completion, was there fear the public wouldn't accept the adoption if known it was DoD/C_A backed?

Do you believe people would join a platform knowing it was under the control of the C_A and FED GOV?

No.

How do you lure the masses into entering all their personal info and private messages (i.e. their LIFE LOG) onto a new platform?

Do you make it cool?

How did FB 'supposedly' start and launch?

Ivy league only?

Develop a trend and/or following?

How do you keep the project running w/o 'public' taxpayer funds? [DoD reported LifeLog was TERMINATED to Congress/Senate OS]

Define 'Black Budget'.

Did HWOOD push?

Do people follow the 'stars'?

Competitors systematically attacked (myspace) to prevent comp?

THE LARGEST 'COLLECTIVE' SOCIAL MEDIA PLATFORM IN THE WORLD (BILLIONS LOGGED) IS OWNED AND OPERATED (COVERTLY) BY THE CENTRAL INTELLIGENCE AGENCY OF THE UNITED STATES OF AMERICA.

The More You Know.

Q

6) The Deep State cannot fully operate without also controlling this world's mainstream media, which it does

What should be clear is that no state, whether communist, a dictatorship, or even a globalist entity, cannot ever be totally be in control over its people unless it controls the media sources that the people will be viewing and listening to. And so, this is also the case for the Deep State, and has been so for many years. That is why President Trump in his tweets on Twitter, and also Q in the Q posts, have been exposing the media as being fake news, over and over again, simply because the Deep State's agenda is to take down President Trump and his administration due to standing in the way of bringing in a one world government.

That there is such willing collusion between the Deep State and this world's mainstream media is clear due to Q identifying such through the word "mockingbird" on the Q posts. Let us notice for instance Q post #113 from November 5, 2017 to begin with:

Owners of Social Media and MSM 113
Anonymous 5 Nov 2017 - 9:53:46 PM
Social media platforms.
Top 10 shareholders of Facebook?
Top 10 shareholders of Twitter?
Top 10 shareholders of Reddit?
Why is SA relevant?
MSM.
Controlling stakes in NBC/MSNBC?
Controlling stakes in ABC?
Controlling stakes in CBS?
Controlling stakes in CNN?
Investor(s) in Fox News?
Why is this relevant?
What is Operation Mockingbird?
Active?
Who is A Cooper?
What is A Cooper's background?
Why is this relevant?
Snow White.

Godfather III.

Speed.

Q

Then let us also note Q post #1822 from August 6, 2018:

Fake News Media = Propaganda Arm of the Democratic Party 1822

Q !A6yxsPKia.6 Aug 2018 - 5:31:41 PM

Psychological Projection.

Define Conspiracy.

1. a secret plan by a group to do something unlawful or harmful.

"a conspiracy to destroy the government"

2. the action of plotting or conspiring.

"they were cleared of conspiracy to pervert the course of justice"

[Fake News]

Fake News collaborating and pushing knowingly false information?

Fake News 'KNOWINGLY FALSE' narrative pushes.

1. POTUS colluded w/ Russia to win the 2016 Presidential election

2. POTUS is puppet to PUTIN

3. POTUS to irreparably harm relationships w/ our allies

4. POTUS will collapse U.S. economy

5. POTUS will collapse stock market

6. POTUS will cause war w/ NK

7. POTUS will cause war w/ IRAN

8. POTUS will destroy the world.

9. On and on……..(knowingly false)

FEAR & SCARE PUSH.

They would rather see NK peace negotiations fail (WAR!) than see POTUS resolve.

Scandalous Media Bias?

Conspiracy?

Collaboration?

What are they hiding?

FAKE NEWS MEDIA IS NOT FREE AND INDEPENDENT.
FAKE NEWS MEDIA = PROPAGANDA ARM OF THE DEMOCRATIC PARTY.
Think WL list of journalists who colluded w/ HRC/DNC (2016 Pres election).
They want you DIVIDED.
DIVIDED by RACE.
DIVIDED by RELIGION.
DIVIDED by CULTURE.
DIVIDED by CLASS.
DIVIDED by POLITICAL AFFILIATION.
DIVIDED YOU ARE WEAK.
TOGETHER YOU ARE STRONG.
YOU, THE PEOPLE, HAVE THE POWER.
This movement challenges their 'forced' narrative.
This movement challenges people to not simply trust what is being reported.
Research for yourself.
Think for yourself.
Trust yourself.
This movement is not about one person or a group of people.
WE, THE PEOPLE.
You are witnessing a FULL PANIC ATTACK by the FAKE NEWS MEDIA & COVERT ALT MEDIA AFFILIATES (foreign gov't).
They cannot contain or defeat what they do not understand.
Is any of this normal?
Think sealed indictments count.
Think resignations of CEOs.
Think resignations of Senators.
Think resignations of Congress.
Think termination of sr FBI…
Think termination of sr DOJ…
WATERGATE X1000
Attacks will only intensify.
Logical thinking.

Ask yourself a simple question – WHY????

Q

And before we move on to the next section, there is one video that readers may find useful to watch on this topic. Video link to: "QAnon - Killing the Mainstream Mockingbird Media "

https://www.youtube.com/watch?v=AHS0UjpM9sE

7) Grasping three possible reasons why God is allowing President Trump, Q, and the Q movement at this time; while at the same time allowing Satan, through the Deep State, to do all that is necessary on earth to bring in a one world government

What we need to grasp in this final section of the present chapter is that God has at least three possible reasons for allowing President Trump, Q, and the Q movement to come on the world scene at the present time; while at the same time allowing Satan, through the Deep State, to do all that is necessary to bring in a one world government in order to prepare the way for the coming antichrist. In other words, this present third age of time will not end and the last seven years remaining of the second age of time will not begin – which is the period of time that Satan, the devil, will be ruling on earth through the antichrist with the aid of the false prophet – until these three events have occurred. What is meant here is that there are at least these three events which must occur on earth before this present third age ends and the antichrist makes his entry on the world scene!

Event #1

God has made it very clear from Romans 11:25-27 that the present third age of time WILL NOT END until all those who are to come to a personal knowledge of God in salvation through faith in His Son, The Lord Jesus Christ, have been saved! So let us note what God there revealed, "[25] For I do not want you, brethren (speaking to believers of the third age, who were not seeing many come to know God in salvation from among the nation of Israel), to be uninformed of this mystery — so that you will not be wise in your own estimation

119

— that a partial hardening has happened to Israel until the fullness of the Gentiles has come in; [26] and so all Israel will be saved; just as it is written, "The Deliverer (God's Son) will come from Zion (in Heaven), He will remove ungodliness from Jacob (Israel)." [27] This is My (new) covenant with them, when I take away their sins" (through the forgiveness of sins in salvation).

And what God means at verse 25 here, when He says to the believers of the third age of time, "a partial hardening has happened to Israel until the fullness of the Gentiles has come in," is that during the present third age of time only some of the nation of Israel are being saved by God's mercy, love, and grace; while the rest remain in unbelief, as those who enter the last seven years remaining of the second age of time as the nation of Israel yet in unbelief (which is the majority of them); with the words "until the fullness of the Gentiles has come in" being a reference to the end of the present third age, with the last of those to be saved by God during the third age having now been saved, which is also the resuming point of the second age of time to complete its last seven years. In other words, when God saves the last person of the present third age to be saved out of the nations of the earth, then He ends the third age by bringing each believer to Heaven (noting 1 Thessalonians 4:14-17) as He removes The Holy Spirit from the earth (noting 2 Thessalonians 2:1-7)!

And so, when God's Son returns from Heaven to earth at the end of the seven years remaining of the second age of time, which is after the third age of time, which is in view at verse 25 here, "all Israel will be saved," at that time, in that all the unbelievers of the earth will have died in the seven years of God's judgment on earth during those seven years, leaving only the believers of the nations of the earth, and also the unbelievers of the nation of Israel as yet alive, since these are elect of God unto salvation, as those who are now saved by God's mercy, grace, and love, who now become part of God's new covenant, as we see above at verse 27 of Romans 11. So we can say here that God's number one agenda then is to see a specific number of Gentiles (non-

Jews) from the nations of the earth come to faith in His Son before He ends the present third age of time!

Event #2)

The second event that God is allowing to occur at this time concerns President Trump, Q, and the Q movement, because again, this is another event that God has allowed at this time in order to cause A GREAT AWAKENING among the nations of the earth! And what is important to grasp here is that this awakening is NOT intended for the believers of the earth, but rather for the unbelievers of the earth! For what needs to be especially grasped here is that when this present third age ends, all the believers of earth – which includes all those awakened by President Trump and Q, AND also all those believers not so awakened – whom God will now remove from the earth in accordance with what He has revealed at 1 Thessalonians 4:14-17 and 2 Thessalonians 2:1-7.

What this further means is that when the above event has occurred, because all those from the Gentile nations have now been saved by God, who are to be saved, then the last seven years of the second age of time resumes to now complete its course, which is when the antichrist now arises on earth over a one world government under the authority and power of the devil. What this further means is that there would not be at that moment any believers on earth, which God soon remedies by saving a multitude of people from among the nations of the earth that no one can count, as we will see later!

And those whom God saves are more than likely those unbelievers of the third age of time, which God had allowed to be awakened by President Trump and Q from the bondage of the Deep State! In other words, there are no coincidences with God, which means that all those unbelievers of the nations of the earth awakened through President Trump and Q at this present time will be all or part of the believers later saved by God at the beginning the last seven years of the second age of time, when the antichrist will be ruling over a one world government on earth. This is a topic we will be revisiting again in Chapter Seven, which deals specifically with this great awakening.

Event #3

Then as to the third event that God is allowing to take place on earth before the present third age ends is letting Satan continue to work through the Deep State, which are the unbelievers of earth bent on seeing a one world government established over the nations of the earth, which require certain necessary components before that can occur. For what we need to grasp here is that for a one world government to be set up, there needs to be a common language for all to be able to understand each other, which would likely be English; then there needs to be a one world currency, that is digitally-based so as to be controllable by that one world government; then there also needs to be a one world religion, which will for sure be the false religious system that the devil first instituted through Cain at the beginning of time, which has Satan as the ultimate object of worship. And so, as earlier mentioned, while the antichrist is the political leader of the coming one world government during those last seven years, the false prophet is leader over the false religious system of earth under the antichrist, with both being under the direct authority and power of Satan, the devil.

And then since the antichrist must be able to completely control a person, in terms of one being able to buy or sell who does not have the mark of the beast, who is the antichrist, on one's right hand or forehead, as we see at Revelation 13:16,17, and since those who will not take that mark of the beast will be the believers of earth that God will have saved at the beginning of the seven years, then that means that we must have in place a system of not only total control over the distribution of perishables, goods, and services, but also a total surveillance system, plus a system for quickly eliminating in death all those who will not submit to the antichrist, by worshipping him or taking his mark as we see at Revelation 13:7.

Many of these systems are now in place, as for instance surveillance cameras, facial recognition technology, being able to locate or track a person anywhere on earth through one's smart phone, or even killing anyone on earth by means of a drone. Plus Artificial Intelligence (AI) has advanced to the point that robots have been made which are so humanlike that it is actually difficult to tell them apart from a live human being!

What this also means then is that we are now in a position to answer the question posed earlier, when we asked how long God will allow President Trump and Q to hold back our slide into the darkness that the Deep State is seeking to pull the whole world into. And now we see that this present third age will not end until all those God wants to bring to faith in His Son have been saved; and President Trump and Q will likely not be removed until God has all those He wants as part of the Great Awakening, and not before, which also ties in to the Deep State needing to be rid of sovereign nations, starting with the United States, before a one world government can be brought in. And lastly, all the tools the antichrist will later need must also be in place before God allows the present third age to end!

So what would be helpful at this point is to give the reader a series of links to videos that will help us see where we are, in terms of how close we are to the end the present third age of time, so that each reader can decide on their own, based on the information provided here. It is highly recommended that each person view the following videos, which have been carefully selected to further enhance the message of this book and of this chapter in particular (and please keep in mind that I am not necessarily advocating or agreeing with all point of view mentioned in the videos).

Link to video, 'The beast system revealed'

https://www.youtube.com/watch?v=21qZUBoLr0U

Link to video, 'They are preparing us for the prince of darkness'

https://www.youtube.com/watch?v=m8HLq4zWq4s

Link to video, 'Biblical beast system rapidly rising'

https://www.youtube.com/watch?v=VVULi9iRHMw

Link to video, 'Unknowingly giving life to the beast system'

https://www.youtube.com/watch?v=X4BN_QbvZQ

Link to video, 'The A.I. takeover is here!'

https://www.youtube.com/watch?v=X8ovlix5fNI

Link to video, 'The scary future of America, 2019-2020'

https://www.youtube.com/watch?v=VP-yweVg2q4

SECTION TWO

IMPORTANT PERSPECTIVES TO BE AWARE OF

"For I know the plans that I have for you,' declares the Lord, 'plans for welfare and not for calamity to give you a future and a hope."

Jeremiah 29:11

CHAPTER FIVE

Trust the plan

While following the Q posts, it was noticed that many of the sayings that were being communicated to followers by Q not only had an immediate application to this present physical world, but also had a very important spiritual component. In other words, President Trump and Q were using terms which were meant to encourage supporters in the ongoing battle of the patriots versus the Deep State in the physical realm of earth; but at the same time these same terms were also found to have a component relating to God and believers in the spiritual realm beyond this earth. And this is now what we will be examining in this second section, as we look at each one of these terms, beginning here in Chapter Five with Q's advice to supporters to 'Trust the plan.'

1) Trust the plan: President Trump, Q, and the Q movement

As will now be seen, in saying, 'Trust the plan,' President Trump and the Q team meant that they had a plan in place, which began even before President Trump announced his candidacy for President on June 15, 2015. So let us begin by noting the video, which is titled, 'We are the plan:'

https://www.youtube.com/watch?v=MRtEgdgj_XQ&list=PL3G PDGjW5SiOnzyvONdfODbjSgZ136nEZ.

That President Trump and Q had a plan is also clear from the following statement on the qmap's global themes, "Q's intel posts (crumbs), which began in October, 2017, will be considered the biggest "inside approved" intel drop in American and world history. Q's posts/crumbs have been carefully prepared and sequenced as part of a 3 year plan. Everything in the crumbs has meaning (everything) -- word choice, topics emphasized, timing, sentence structure, misspellings, etc. Q's crumbs combined equate the Map and Plan. The crumbs are intentionally cryptic to throw off bad actors and conceal strategic moves. The news cycle unlocks the map and the crumbs begin to make sense -- future (news) proves the past (Q posts). Trust the plan and enjoy the show!"

The following two Q posts also speak about President Trump and the Q team having such a plan in place, noting first Q post #1332 from May 10, 2018:

Stay the Course and Trust the Plan 1332
Q !4pRcUA0Lbe 10 May 2018 - 8:43:20 PM
Fellow Patriots:
What you are about to learn should not only scare you, but intensify your resolve to take back control [Freedom]. The information that will become public will further demonstrate the criminal & corrupt [pure evil] abuse of power that the Hussein administration undertook in joint efforts w/ domestic and foreign dignitaries. The snowball has begun rolling - there is no stopping it now. D5.
Stay the course and trust the plan.
Protective measures are in place.
Remain BRAVE.
We knew this day would come.
https://www.youtube.com/watch?v=G2qIXXafxCQ■
United We Stand (WW).
WWG1WGA.
We FIGHT.
Conspiracy no more.
Q

And then also noting Q post #2937 from March 3, 2019:

This Is a Methodical Plan Moving Ahead Step by Step with Military Precision 2937

Q !!mG7VJxZNCl 3 Mar 2019 - 12:27:22 PM

Why have there been no arrests?

Why have 'specific' dates been mentioned only to see no action?

Define 'game theory'.

Why must disinformation be provided?

Define 'open source'.

Define 'public purview'.

Do we let our enemies walk through the front door?

Define 'plausible deniability'.

Why was it important to FIRST clean house within the FBI & DOJ (public info)?

Why was it important to FIRST clean house within other ABC agencies (non_public info)?

What are the duties of the FBI?

What are the duties of the DOJ?

When does MIL INTEL have jurisdiction?

What vested powers does POTUS have re: MIL INTEL vs. ABC agencies re: matters of NAT SEC (HOMELAND)?

Think 'umbrella surv'.

What agency does the FBI report to?

What is the role of the AG?

Does the AG oversee the firing of FBI & DOJ senior/mid/lower staff?

How many FBI & DOJ were FIRED/FORCED?

Does 'Russia' recusal prevent/block AG from this responsibility?

What time period did this occur?

Who appointed and tasked HUBER?

Who appointed and tasked the OIG?

Who was AG?

[zero leaks - none]

Transfer from AG1 to AG2?

Why might that be important?

How do you avoid 'politically motivated/attack - obstruction - attempt to block/obstruct Mueller'?

Optics are important.

When are optics not important?

Think Whitaker.

Define 'stage set'.

Who recently walked 'on stage' to take command?

What 'stage' experience did this person have?

Think Bill Clinton impeachment.

Has the 'stage' been cleaned & cleared for the next performance?

If the 'stage' is clean, can the performance begin?

How might 'transparency' [DECLAS] fit into the dialogue?

Define 'thesis' statement.

What benefit(s) does this provide BARR?

"This is not simply another four-year election. This is a crossroads in the history of our civilization that will determine whether or not we, the people, reclaim control over our government." - POTUS

Logical thinking.

Q

2) Trust the plan: God and believers

And what we now need to observe is that while President Trump and the Q team have a plan to defeat the Deep State in its visible aspects on earth, in order to restore power to the people of the United States and other countries of the earth, nevertheless all hinges on God's own plan that He is outworking through the four ages of time! So while one discovers that President Trump and the Q team have a plan when one first becomes cognizant of Q and the Q movement, and then one learns to trust that plan from becoming a follower; similarly with God. When we first come into a personal relationship with God in salvation, we discover from reading His word that He too has a plan for those who believe in His Son, as is clear from Jeremiah 29:11, "For I know the plans that I have for you,' declares the Lord, 'plans for welfare and not for calamity to give you a future and a hope."

Then as we become followers of God after salvation, we discover that God also calls His own to trust Him, as we see at Proverbs 3:5,6, "Trust in the LORD with all your heart And do not lean on your own understanding. In all your ways acknowledge Him, And He will make your paths straight," simply because we can trust His eternal plan for us beyond this life, which is not just for time, but for all eternity, noting for instance what God also promises believers at 1 Corinthians 2:9, but just as it is written, "THINGS WHICH EYE HAS NOT SEEN AND EAR HAS NOT HEARD, AND WHICH HAVE NOT ENTERED THE HEART OF MAN, ALL THAT GOD HAS PREPARED FOR THOSE WHO LOVE HIM.""

"Do I have any pleasure in the death of the wicked," declares the Lord GOD, "rather than that he should turn from his ways and live?"

Ezekiel 18:23

"And inasmuch as it is appointed for men to die once and after this comes judgment."

Hebrews 9:27

CHAPTER SIX

The calm before the storm

1) The calm before the storm: President Trump, Q, and the Q movement

Whereas the previous statement on 'trust the plan' was said to the Q patriots, this is not the case, however, in regards to the term that we will look at in this chapter, which is 'the calm before the storm.' What we are to grasp here then is that this statement was first made by President Trump in a public setting on October 5th, 2017, while holding formal meetings with military officers at the White House, with this particular statement being a direct warning to the Deep State! As one can see from the following video of that occasion, the mainstream media immediately picked up on this statement and at that moment and in the days following kept asking what it meant. So let us note the video, which is titled, 'The Second American Revolution is Underway:'

https://www.youtube.com/watch?v=j1rjiJgM8_g

Then shortly after that, on November 1, 2017, Q made the first mention of the phrase, 'the calm before the storm' in Q post #38, which was three days after the Q posts started:

The Calm Before the Storm 38
Anonymous 1 Nov 2017 - 11:48:52 PM
Four carriers & escorts in the pacific?
Why is that relevant?

To prevent other state actors from attempting to harm us during this transition? Russia / China?

Or conversely all for NK? Or all three.

Think logically about the timing of everything happening.

Note increased military movement.

Note NG deployments starting tomorrow.

Note false flags.

Follow Huma.

Prepare messages of reassurance based on what was dropped here to spread on different platforms.

The calm before the storm.

And even though the anons and patriots had heard the statement 'the calm before the storm' from President Trump on October 5, 2017, and then from Q on November 1, 2017, it nevertheless caused a certain measure of impatience in the Q movement. For many had interpreted the statement as meaning that at some point soon, all the criminals involved in the Deep State would be arrested. So as we neared the end of 2018 and that had not yet happened, since President Trump had not yet declassified the damaging information relating to Deep State that was still being held as 'classified,' it led one anon to ask Q about that statement on December 3, 2018, noting now Q post #2546 and Q's answer:

23 Days Delta Between POTUS 'The Calm Before the Storm' and the First Q Post 2546

Q !!mG7VJxZNCI 3 Dec 2018 - 3:41:45 PM

Anonymous 3 Dec 2018 - 3:37:53 PM

>>4134775

Okay. Is the plot moving forward? I think we all understand the characters and conflict at this point. Time for the plot twist? Declas, FINALLY?

>>4134817

The President of the United States initiated and confirmed the order when he stated "The Calm Before the Storm."

When was the statement made?

When did "Q" go active?

Watch the News.

Watch the FBI.

Watch the DOJ.

Q

What Q was indicating is that 'the storm' could not proceed until all was in place, such as removing all the corrupt people in the FBI and DOJ, plus gathering all the information and evidence in sealed indictments (which one can view on the Qmap, that being the third tag from the bottom on the left sidebar), which was 'the calm before the storm.' Only then could the storm proceed, which was all the prosecutions of those in the Deep State! So this brings us back to 'Trust the plan,' which is the three year plan put in place by President Trump and military intelligence that they are working in accordance with in order to take down the Deep State and all the leading characters worldwide. And as one can gather, who has followed Q for any length of time, this is something that not only takes time, but is fraught with danger, as the Deep State will not stop at anything or for anyone in order to retain global control, even if thousands, or even millions, of people have to suffer or die!

What many observed, who were closely following the Q posts, is that since Q spoke of the plan being carried out over three years, then this meant that it would be in three phases. In order words, Phase 1 would be operations to cut all the Deep State strings, while Phase 2 would be continuing on with Phase 1 while gathering all the evidence and building cases against those key players of the Deep State. So this meant that Phase 1 and 2 would be part of 'the calm,' while the 'the storm' would then be Phase 3, which would involve the prosecution and putting an end to these Deep State players. That this is so can be gathered from some of the Q posts. So let us notice Q post 243 from December 30, 2017, where Q mentioned what was being done in Phase 1:

Saudi Arabia Controlled US Politicians 243
Q !ITPb.qbhqo 30 Nov 2017 - 10:17:43 PM
SA controlled US puppets.
Strings cut.
D's dropping all around over sexual misconduct (1st stage).

Coincidence directly after SA?

Don't you realize the war has gone public?

List who will not be running for re_election.

Coincidence?

Phase I.

Easy to swallow.

Loss of power/influence.

Good time to prosecute.

Just wait until next week.

You are all Patriots.

Q

Then let us notice Q post #797 from February 20, 2018, where Q indicated that Phase 2 was then in progress:

POTUS Phase 2 Marker 797

Q !UW.yye1fxo 20 Feb 2018 - 11:44:40 PM

Stay tuned.

Everything has meaning or a purpose.

@Jack - getting nervous?

Phase [2].

Q

And then thirdly, let us notice Q post #2724 from February 14, 2019, which is almost one year later, where Q now mentions that Phase 3 is about to begin, which is 'the storm' in view in the statement 'the calm before the storm:'

Phase III: A Traitor's Justice 2724

Q !!mG7VJxZNCI 14 Feb 2019 - 9:42:27 PM

A Traitor's Justice.

Phase III

Panic in DC.

RATS EVERYWHERE.

For those who decide to save the taxpayers some money - There is no escaping God.

Q

2) The calm before the storm: God and unbelievers

And so, just as the statement 'the calm before the storm,' as coming from President Trump and Q was meant as a warning to the Deep State, in terms of justice coming for them; so too are we to now see the statement 'the calm before the storm' as also applying spiritually to all the unbelievers of this world, in that there is God's justice coming for them, which is His judgment! What this further means is that just as many were freed from their being puppets to the Deep State by agreeing to help President Trump (one example being Senator Lindsay Graham of South Carolina), then too unbelievers of this world can also be free from ever facing God's judgment and hell, if they believe the gospel during their time on earth, with that gospel being the good news that God has made known in His word at 1 Corinthians 15:1-4 regarding His Son, The Lord Jesus Christ.

And so, for all unbelievers of this world, 'the calm' is the duration of their life here on earth during which time they are all given an opportunity by God to believe in His Son, and thereby be able to escape 'the storm,' which is God's judgment and the eternal fire of hell, which is only for those who refuse to believe in God's Son for the forgiveness of sins and the reception of eternal life before physical death comes! And of course, for believers, there is never any 'storm,' as is also true for the patriots now following President Trump and Q.

"But we do not want you to be uninformed, brethren, about those who are asleep, so that you will not grieve as do the rest who have no hope. For if we believe that Jesus died and rose again, even so God will bring with Him those who have fallen asleep in Jesus. For this we say to you by the word of the Lord, that we who are alive and remain until the coming of the Lord, will not precede those who have fallen asleep. For the Lord Himself will descend from heaven with a shout, with the voice of the archangel and with the trumpet of God, and the dead in Christ will rise first. Then we who are alive and remain will be caught up together with them in the clouds to meet the Lord in the air, and so we shall always be with the Lord. Therefore comfort one another with these words."

1 Thessalonians 4:13-18

CHAPTER SEVEN

Where we go one we go all (WWG1WGA)

1) Where we go one we go all: President Trump, Q, and the Q movement

Another saying which soon became a rallying cry by the Q movement is the adoption by President Trump and Q of the statement made in the 1996 Ridley Scott movie, 'White Squall,' starring Jeff Bridges, 'Where we go one we go all,' also sometimes abbreviated as 'WWG1WGA.' Let us notice for instance Q post #1621 from June 28, 2018, where Q mentions the origin of the statement:

WWG1WGA Origin: White Squall Movie (1996) 1621
Q !CbboFOtcZs 28 Jun 2018 - 10:33:42 AM
We remember you, Mr. VIP!
https://mobile.twitter.com/Q_ANONBaby/status/10122329946
46581248◼
WWG1WGA!
Where did the Storm derive from?
Some things leave lasting impressions.
Listen carefully.
https://m.youtube.com/watch?v=B5T7Gr5oJbM&feature=yout
u.be◼
When did POTUS make the statement?
When did we arrive to start the awakening?
You have more than you know.
Fireworks.

Q

Then let us notice Q post #2544 from December 3, 2018, where Q gave the trailer to the movie 'White Squall:'

White Squall 1996 Movie Trailer 2544

Q !!mG7VJxZNCI 3 Dec 2018 - 3:35:39 PM

https://www.youtube.com/watch?v=B5T7Gr5oJbM&feature=y outu.be■

Q

And before we comment further on this, let us view the trailer: https://www.youtube.com/watch?v=B5T7Gr5oJbM&feature=y outu.be. So what the statement 'where we go one we go all' came to mean in the Q movement then was that President Trump, Q, and the Q followers were all in this together, just as in the movie; for all those gathered in the schooner were working together on that ship, so that when that white squall hit, they would all sink or survive together! And so too with all those who become Q followers; one cannot just sit on the fence and just be an observer in the Q movement, as one soon finds that one becomes deeply involved in what is going on worldwide as a result of the Q post information being shared. And now, let us close this section with a song written and sung by J.T. Wilde with the title, 'WWG1WGA:' https://www.youtube.com/watch?v=KXNiBMlxl7g

2) Where we go one we go all: God, believers, and unbelievers

And then from the spiritual standpoint, we could easily see that the statement, WWG1WGA, also applies to all believers of the earth, as is clear from the quote from 1 Thessalonians 4:13-18 to begin this present chapter, for when God's Son, The Lord Jesus Christ, returns at the first stage of His second coming to just above the earth to remove all the believers of this present third age, both those who have died already and those who are still alive, then it is clear that we will all be taken at once, with none being left behind. In other words, the statement 'where we go one we go all' will definitely then apply to all believers of the present third age of time, as we all at once and together will be leaving this earth to be with God in Heaven forever!

And of course the same is true also for all the unbelievers of the four ages of time, for when God's final judgment comes as time ends and eternity begins, as we see at Revelation 20:11-15, then all the unbelievers of time will be raised from the dead (for all will have died, noting Hebrews 9:27) to face God at that final judgment before being cast by Him into the lake of fire, which is eternal hell, due to none of them having believed in God's Son, The Lord Jesus Christ, during their stay on earth. What this further means then is that the statement 'where we go one we go all' will also at that time be seen to apply to all unbelievers of the four ages of time!

Jesus said to His followers at Mark 9:40, "fort whoever is not against us is for us."

CHAPTER EIGHT

The great awakening

1) The great awakening: President Trump, Q, and the Q movement

Another statement often seen in the Q posts and heard among those in the Q movement is the phrase, the 'Great Awakening.' Let us note a couple of early Q posts in that regard, first Q post #164 from November 20, 2017, which was less than one month from when the Q posts started on October 28, 2017:

The Great Awakening is Spreading 164
Q !ITPb.qbhqo 20 Nov 2017 - 2:05:24 AM
Bots deactivated upon arrival.
Keep up the good fight.
It's spreading.
Q

And then let us notice Q post #289 of December 6, 2017, where we see that the news about the Q posts was starting to spread further and further afield, even becoming worldwide:

Great Awakening Spreading Exponentially 289
Q !ITPb.qbhqo 6 Dec 2017 - 10:33:36 PM
Reached est 1.2mm, Patriots.
You are reaching more than you know.
1=2, 2=4, 4=8, …

Godspeed.

Q

And so, what we are now to grasp is that the 'Great Awakening' for President Trump, Q, and the Q movement concerns all the people of the nations of the earth having their eyes opened to the fact of there being a Deep State at work in this world, which is not only seeking to establish a one world government, but is bent on keeping all human beings of earth under its control. In other words, one of the prime goals of President Trump and Q is not only to bring down the Deep State and its key players, but to also open the eyes of the general population worldwide, through the information being provided in the Q posts, so that people everywhere might know what is really happening now, and also what has really happened so far in modern history, which is definitely not in accordance with what we were taught in school.

2) The great awakening: God and believers

Then we are also to be aware that spiritually speaking, a 'Great Awakening' refers to a revival, as when unbelievers in large numbers are awakened from their unbelief to believe in God's Son for the forgiveness of sins and the reception of eternal life. One such 'Great Awakening' occurred in England and its thirteen colonies in the decade between 1730 and 1740 under the preaching of George Whitefield, John Wesley, and Jonathan Edwards. What is also noteworthy is that this spiritual 'Great Awakening' went beyond existing denominational lines at the time, so that God was doing a mighty work among all classes of people, no matter what level of education, amount of wealth, skin color, or gender.

And what is very important for us to note now, further to what was mentioned when looking at Event #2 in Chapter Four, is that at the present time, believers who are part of the Q movement do not need a 'Great Awakening' per se, in that most are already aware that Satan controls this present world system and that there is a Deep State on earth in the physical realm doing his bidding, along with a slew of demons also in the spiritual world around us. That is why so many believers were already Trump supporters, even before Q started, simply because they knew that the election of Hilary Clinton would have likely meant the end of the United States as we know it.

What this means then is that the 'Great Awakening' also has another very important spiritual component at the present time. What is meant here is that many people who are being awakened to the truth being shared by Q at the present time, and who then become followers as part of the Q movement, are great numbers of UNBELIEVERS worldwide. It is true that many of these are coming to know God, since these are having contact with many others in the Q movement who are already believers. However, many of those who will further be awakened in the 'Great Awakening,' when Q fully makes known all the hidden information on the Deep State, may not become believers in God now, but may later.

What is meant here is that for an unbeliever at the present time to make a stand AGAINST Satan and the devil signifies that one is making a stand WITH God. And let us note what God's Son said to His followers at Mark 9:40, "fort whoever is not against us is for us." And so, in unbelievers taking a stand against the devil and the Deep State through the 'Great Awakening' at this time means that they are therefore to be seen as definitely taking a stand for God, for what needs to be further realized here is that what Q is doing is sharing the truth and exposing the lies of the Deep State! In other words, to stand for Q is not only to stand for truth, but it is also to stand for good against evil, which is really the battle that has been raging in both the physical realm of earth and in the spiritual realm beyond us since the time of Adam and Ever the garden of Eden.

So let us hold that thought for a moment and let us move on to speak of what happens if millions upon millions of people, that being especially unbelievers, are awakened to the truth, as is indeed presently occurring, and God decides to bring the present third age to an end, as is very much possible and widely expected. That would mean, as earlier indicated, that we would immediately have the removal of all believers from the earth, as the last seven years of the second age of time now resumes to bring it to a completion, which is when the antichrist arises over the nations of the earth and establishes a one world government, assisted by the false prophet, who now leads a one world religion, with both being under the authority and power of Satan, the devil, during this seven year period.

And what concerns us here are all those unbelievers who are on earth and who had taken their stand against Satan and the Deep State before this present age ended. In other words, the 'Great Awakening' of all these unbelievers at the present time may mean that they are the ones that God saves at the beginning of when that seven year period begins, as when the antichrist will be on earth, for it is clear from Revelation 7, which speaks of that seven year period, that God will indeed save a multitude of people on earth, noting for instance Revelation 7:9,10, "After these things I looked, and behold, a great multitude which no one could count, from every nation and all tribes and peoples and tongues, standing before the throne and before the Lamb, clothed in white robes, and palm branches were in their hands; and they cry out with a loud voice, saying, " Salvation to our God who sits on the throne, and to the Lamb." "

From Revelation 7:13,14 we learn that those in view at verses 9 and 10 just quoted above came out of the great tribulation, as we now see, "Then one of the elders answered, saying to me, "These who are clothed in the white robes, who are they, and where have they come from?" I said to him, "My lord, you know." And he said to me, "These are the ones who come out of the great tribulation, and they have washed their robes and made them white in the blood of the Lamb." What we are to observe here is that "the great tribulation" in view here is the last three and a half years of that coming seven year period, which is when the false prophet, as leader over the false religious system of earth will be assisting the antichrist, who is the political leader over the nations of the earth.

And it is during that last three and a half years that the false prophet sets up an image of the antichrist and causes people on earth to worship the image, as is clear from Revelation 13:14,15, with those who refuse being killed, as is clear from what we there read, "And he (the false prophet) deceives those who dwell on the earth because of the signs which it was given him to perform in the presence of the beast (who is the antichrist), telling those who dwell on the earth to make an image to the beast who had the wound of the sword and has come to life. And it was given to him to give breath to the image of the beast, so that the image of the beast would even speak and cause as many as do not worship the image of the beast to be killed."

Those who will be killed here will be the believers that God will have saved at the beginning of that seven year period, which are in view at Revelation 7:9,10,13,14. And as already mentioned, those believers will most likely be drawn from those unbelievers who were awakened during the Great Awakening of Q and the Q movement of the present time; but since they were still in unbelief when the this present third age ended they remained on the earth to be saved by God only at the beginning of that seven year period.

That there are believers on earth during that first half of the last seven years left of the second age of time is also clear from what God tells us at Revelation 13:7,8, "It was also given to him (that is, the antichrist) to make war with the saints (the believers that God will have saved at the beginning of that seven year period) and to overcome them, and authority over every tribe and people and tongue and nation was given to him. All who dwell on the earth will worship him, everyone whose name has not been written from the foundation of the world in the book of life of the Lamb who has been slain." And so, it is clear that there are believers that arise in the first half of the seven years during the time the antichrist will be ruling over a one world government here on earth, and the point being made here again is that those believers are most likely drawn from those unbelievers of the present third age, who are awakened during the 'Great Awakening" of Q and the Q movement, but who remain unbelievers as this present age ends, being only saved by God early on as the seven last years of the second age resumes!

"Woe to those who call evil good, and good evil;
Who substitute darkness for light and light for
darkness…"

Isaiah 5:20 in part

"to open their eyes so that they may turn from
darkness to light and from the dominion of Satan to
God, that they may receive forgiveness of sins and
an inheritance among those who have been
sanctified by faith in Me."

Acts 26:18

CHAPTER NINE

/ Darkness to light

1) Darkness to light: President Trump, Q, and the Q movement

Another phrase that Q often uses to end Q posts is 'darkness to light,' or simply 'dark to light.' Here are a few examples from the Q posts, noting first Q post #328 of December 11, 2017:

Light Will Overcome Darkness 328
Q !ITPb.qbhqo 11 Dec 2017 - 10:32:11 AM
:Owls:
Light will overcome d_a_rkness.
Light will expose darkne_s_s.
Light will _reveal_ darkness.
Light will defeat darkness.
Q

And then let us also note Q post #1440 of June 3:2018:

Dark to Light Marker 1440
Q !CbboFOtcZs 3 Jun 2018 - 1:58:29 PM
BOOM.
  BOOM.
    BOOM.
      BOOM.

A WEEK TO REMEMBER.
DARK TO LIGHT.
BLACKOUT NECESSARY.
Q

And again, let us note the very revealing Q post #2573 of December 10, 2018:

John F. Kennedy Quote on Dark to Light 2573
Q !!mG7VJxZNCl 10 Dec 2018 - 12:47:08 PM
"The times are too grave, the challenge too urgent, and the stakes too high — to permit the customary passions of political debate. We are not here to curse the darkness, but to light the candle that can guide us through that darkness to a safe and sane future."
—JFK
Q

It is clear from the above quote that President John F Kennedy was out to bring light to the United States and by extension to the world, in terms of exposing the Deep State, which is one reason he was assassinated. Here is a revealing quote from the Q map themes section in this regard, "Presidents John F Kennedy (JFK), Ronald Reagan, and Donald Trump are all different than the rest (outliers). The election "fix" has been in -- no matter which party (D's or R's) won. They assassinated JFK, shot Reagan, and undoubtedly tried to do the same to Trump. These Presidents could not be controlled and therefore represented a threat. With President Trump and our mighty military, they (that is, the Deep State) are now facing an existential threat like never before."

And so, just as the 'Great Awakening' in the previous section related to the people of the world being awakened one by one to the truth being shared by President Trump and Q, now we are to see that 'dark to light' relates primarily to the darkness of this world as a whole being pushed back as

President Trump, Q, and the Q movement spread the truth throughout the United States and the world, for light dispels the darkness as surely as truth dispels lies!

But there is one concern which needs to be mentioned here, which is that as Q exposes people to the evil that lurks in that darkness, this means that there are many people who are now in contact with that evil, which had before been unknown, especially as one examines various sites on the internet to find out more, since we are all naturally curious by nature. And the danger here is especially for those believers who may not be well grounded in the word of God and the faith, who may be duly affected in terms of not knowing how to incorporate this information into their daily lives. And the same to some extent would be true even among those who are not yet believers. This is where those who are more mature will have to be on the lookout around them to help those who need help to incorporate this information and to go on living life as normally as possible in an increasingly abnormal world that the enemy of our souls tries to keep fostering upon us!

2) Darkness to light: God and believers

And when we come to look at this phrase 'darkness to light' from a spiritual standpoint, we are to realize that all that occurs in this world is not in accordance with the military intelligence and planning operating behind President Trump and Q in bringing light to the world in order to dispel the darkness, but rather this world is under God's direct control at all times, including the present. What is meant here is that in accordance with God's plan already indicated in Chapter Three, there will be darkness like human beings on earth have never known it before, which will be for seven years, as soon as this present third age of time ends.

For we need to remember that even though President Trump and Q may bring much light to dispel the darkness caused by Satan through the Deep State on earth at the present time, nevertheless, the reality is that this light of the present time will soon be replaced by seven years of unimaginable darkness, for the antichrist will by ruling over the nations of the earth, as assisted by the false prophet as religious leader of the false world religion, with both being under the direct control and authority of Satan, the devil. And so, it is only at the end of that seven years of the reign of the antichrist that God's light will come to this world to dispel the darkness, which will occur with God's Son now coming to earth again in the second stage of His second coming. And then, and only then, will the darkness be dispelled from the earth and be replaced with the light of God for the next thousand years, which is the duration of the fourth age of time!

"Now to Him who is able to do far more abundantly beyond all that we ask or think…"

Ephesians 3:20 in part

CHAPTER TEN

/ All depends upon President Trump

1) All depends on President Trump

Those who have been aware of what has been going on since Mr Trump announced his candidacy for President of the United States on June 16, 2015, are no doubt astounded that the man is even still going on; still fighting for the truth and for restoring power back to the people. At no time in history has a mere human being endured so much hate and abuse at the hands of fellow human beings! Not only has the mainstream media not been reporting all that has been accomplished so far by the Trump Administration, but it is even a wonder that anything has been done at all, since many even in his own Republican party oppose him at almost every turn! One recent example is that the Republican-held Senate cannot even side in his National Emergency Declaration in order to build a wall at the southern border to stem the flow of illegal immigrants, and drug, human, and gun traffickers. It is no exaggeration to say that at no time in history has so many freedom-loving people on earth looked to one man! And at the same time, at no time in history has so many unbelievers of earth looked for one man to lead them, which will turn out to be the antichrist!

Let us note a few Q posts here to amplify the truth that President Trump is indeed a unique human being at this time in history, noting for example Q post #153 of November 14, 2017:

Why Donald Trump 153

Q !ITPb.qbhqo 14 Nov 2017 - 7:25:09 PM

For the coming days ahead.

Ask yourself an honest question, why would a billionaire who has it all, fame, fortune, a warm and loving family, friends, etc. want to endanger himself and his family by becoming POTUS?

Why would he want to target himself and those he cares about?

Does he need money?

Does he need fame?

What does he get out of this?

Does he want to make the US/world a better place for his family and for those good and decent people who have long been taken advantage of?

Perhaps he could not stomach the thought of mass murders occurring to satisfy Moloch?

Perhaps he could not stomach the thought of children being kidnapped, drugged, and raped while leaders/law enforcement of the world turn a blind eye.

Perhaps he was tired of seeing how certain races/countries were being constantly abused and kept in need/poor/and suffering all for a specific purpose.

Perhaps he could not in good conscious see the world burn.

Why, hours after the election, did seven people travel to an undisclosed location to hold a very private & highly secured/guarded meeting?

Why didn't HRC give a concession speech?

When was the last time a presidential candidate didn't personally give a concession speech?

What happens if the border remained open and the MSM continued to brainwash?

At what point do Patriots, and hard working men and woman, become the minority?

What about voting machines?

Who owns the voting machines?

What about voter ID laws?

Photo ID? When is it necessary and must be presented? Make a list. Laugh.

Reconcile.

Would the chances of defeating evil grow less and less with each passing year?

What does 'red line' mean?

Why, again, were the arrests made in SA so very important?

What strings were immediately cut?

Follow the money.

When does a bird sing?

Q

The same sentiment was expressed again, albeit more briefly a little over a year later, in Q post #2553 of December 5, 2018:

President Trump Risked Everything to Fight For & Defend We, the PEOPLE 2553

Q !!mG7VJxZNCl 5 Dec 2018 - 11:27:19 AM

Anonymous

5 Dec 2018 - 10:56:46 AM

Screen Shot 2018-12-05 at 9.53.35 AM.png

POTUS FLOTUS not participating in this evil.

>>4166910

One man, who gave up everything, risking his life (himself/family), to fight for & defend, We, the PEOPLE.

Bait expends ammunition.

EVIL has no place here.

Q

And then let us note that a week later, an anon asked Q a relevant question for our present purpose, which is Q post #2609 of December 12, 2018:

Q Has Plan for After Trump's Presidency 2609

Q !!mG7VJxZNCl 12 Dec 2018 - 4:43:49 PM

Anonymous

12 Dec 2018 - 4:43:32 PM

>>4280189

Is there a plan in place for AFTER trump?

>>4280228

Yes.

Q

As we see above, there is a plan in place for after President Trump. Whether that means after he serves two terms or not, we do not know. But as we will now see below, it does not really matter.

2) All depends on God

As was mentioned when looking at President Trump in Chapter One, he would not be in power today if it was not for God, and he likely would not have been protected from all harm either apart from God's protection, since there have been multiple attempts on his life already, and that is only the ones that have been made public! We really need to grasp and hold to the reality that all really does depend on God, who not only controls life, but also death itself. In other words, no one is ever born into this world unless God allows it and no one dies unless God allows it.

What this means then is that President Trump will continue until he has served the purpose of God in his own generation, as is true for any human being born into this world in time, noting what God says at Acts 13:36, "For David (the name of any human being can be inserted here), after he had served the purpose of God in his own generation, fell asleep (that is, he died), and was laid among his fathers and underwent decay." For as we have seen in Chapter Four, when discussing the three events (at the least) there that God was working towards before He will bring this present third age of time to a close, those being again in short: 1) To save all those whom God wanted to save during this present third age of time; 2) To use President Trump, Q, and the Q movement to awaken people worldwide at this present time, with God then saving the unbelieving portion at the beginning of the last seven years left of the second age of time; and 3) That world conditions needing to be brought to the place that God can allow the devil to bring in his antichrist over a one world government and his false prophet over a one world religion. And so we see that ultimately, all depends on God!

SECTION THREE

THINGS FOR BELIEVERS TO GUARD AGAINST AND TO DO

"You will know them by their fruits…"

Matthew 7:16 in part

CHAPTER ELEVEN

Let us guard against labeling President Trump as a non-Christian!

What we will be doing in this third section is point out certain things that believers need to guard against and do relating to President Trump, Q, and the Q movement in the light of the times we live in. And in regards to this present chapter, the first thing that believers need to guard against is labeling President Trump as a not being a true believer. What is especially sad here is that I have seen three supposedly Christian YouTube channels pointing a finger at President Trump and declaring to the world that he was not a Christian. In these videos, President Trump was shown in all kinds of situations during his past life as proof that he was not a true believer. The reality to be grasped here is that none should be judged based on one's past life, but on one's present life, if one is to be judged at all. For even those who are true believers now were not Christians either before coming to know God through faith in His precious Son!

The reason Matthew 7:16, where God says, "You shall know them by their fruits...," was chosen as a quote for this chapter is that this part verse is very much applicable in President Trump's case. Whether President Trump is a believer or not, only God knows for sure. But this we do know, is that God gave us the verse to let us know that we would know true believers by the life that is lived after coming to personally God through faith in His Son. And it is undeniable to anyone who has followed Mr Trump since declaring his candidacy for

President that he has run an honest campaign, with no one having come forth yet with some wrongdoing that could be proven true. Even under extreme stress, he has set a moral example for all.

Before we comment further on this subject, let us note a number of videos relating to Mr Trump, beginning with this one, titled, 'Recognizing God's Hand in Donald Trump's election' (with a disclaimer here that I am not advocating for any website, or necessarily any views expressed outside of the fact that God has indeed been at work in the recent life of President Trump. In other words, the purpose of showing these video clips is to prove that there is 'fruit' here): https://www.youtube.com/watch?v=aRcnJPQqY0c

Here are two other videos where President Trump declares his stand for religious freedom and Biblical values:

https://www.youtube.com/watch?v=FWTQgl4VSEY

https://www.youtube.com/watch?v=HmmW6Q1oLfM

And here are three videos where President Trump asks someone to pray, the first is at a cabinet meeting, where Vice President Mike Pence also thanks President Trump for keeping his promises to the people of the United States; the second video is where President Trump asks a minister to pray before starting a White House meeting; and same with the third one. And let us remember that all these videos are with the national media being present!

https://www.youtube.com/watch?v=DQDzCbAHwFY

https://www.youtube.com/watch?v=b4itRBfSJhM

https://www.youtube.com/watch?v=a0_mCivoTSs

Now here are two videos where someone asks President Trump if they can pray for him, and he consents, keeping in mind that both of these are before the national media. The first video is at this year's National Prayer Breakfast; while the second is when President Trump welcomed a winning football team to the White House:

https://www.youtube.com/watch?v=US9nlaVF9ZM

https://www.youtube.com/watch?v=42nK8wo_fwE

Let us keep in mind what God's Son told His disciples at Luke 9:26, "For whoever is ashamed of Me and My words, the Son of Man will be ashamed of him when He comes in His glory, and the glory of the Father and of the holy angels." From the above videos, it is obvious that President Trump is definitely not ashamed to associate with Bible-believing Christians, or to have them pray for him, and that before a national audience! And with that in mind, let us note what President Trump told a graduating class in 2017, especially being attentive to his frequent references to God and faith in Him, https://www.youtube.com/watch?v=Rpfkh1HLsiE

As we come to close this chapter, it is worth mentioning that I have personally heard of two nationally-known evangelical leaders who have publicly stated that they believed that President Trump was a Christian. One is Jerry Falwell, Jr, who is the President of Liberty University in Lynchburg, Virginia, who stated so while introducing Mr. Trump to the student body at the university. I personally heard him say this live online, but have searched online for a video of this while writing this book and cannot find a link for readers here. The other is Dr James Dobson, who started the ministry 'Focus on the Family.' Here is an article that appeared in the New York Times on June 25, 2016 (the reason that the link is not being given to the article itself is that they want you to subscribe, as content is not free):

A Born-Again Donald Trump? Believe It, Evangelical Leader Says

By Trip Gabriel and Michael Luo, June 25, 2016

Has Donald J. Trump become a born-again Christian?

That is the suggestion of James C. Dobson, one of America's leading evangelicals, who said Mr. Trump had recently come "to accept a relationship with Christ" and was now "a baby Christian."

Dr. Dobson, the founder of Focus on the Family and one of the country's most prominent social conservatives, gave his account at a meeting Mr. Trump had in New York on Tuesday with hundreds of Christian conservatives.

In an interview recorded at the event by a Pennsylvania pastor, the Rev. Michael Anthony (see link below this article), Dr. Dobson said he knew the person who had led Mr. Trump to Christ, though he did not name him. "I don't know when it was, but it has not been long," Dr. Dobson said. "I believe he really made a commitment, but he's a baby Christian."

Mr. Anthony posted the interview to his blog on Friday. Dr. Dobson could not be reached on Saturday, and Hope Hicks, the Trump campaign spokeswoman, did not respond Saturday to a request for details.

Mr. Trump stumbled at times last year when speaking about faith. At one point he said that he had never asked for God's forgiveness. And after repeating on the campaign trail that the Bible was his favorite book, ahead of his own "Art of the Deal," Mr. Trump declined to name a favorite verse. "The Bible means a lot to me, but I don't want to get into specifics," he told Bloomberg Television.

Mr. Trump, a Presbyterian, questioned the faith of Hillary Clinton, a Methodist, at a meeting with a smaller group of evangelical leaders on Tuesday, saying, "We don't know anything about Hillary in terms of religion."

During the New York meeting, Mr. Trump made no mention of being born again. It is a possibility certain to cause chortles in some corners, but it could also open doors in others for the thrice-married presumptive Republican nominee for president.

For evangelicals, "accepting Christ" is at the heart of becoming a genuine Christian, and refers to acknowledging sin and declaring the need for Jesus Christ as savior. "The expectation evangelicals have is of a radical change, a 180-degree turn from the life of sin to following Christ," said Kedron Bardwell, a political science professor at Simpson College in Iowa, who is the son of an evangelical pastor.

With new believers, this is often done in prayer with another Christian, which may have been what Dr. Dobson was referring to when he said that he knew the person who had "led him to Christ."

Mr. Trump won a majority of evangelical voters in the Republican primaries, though some prominent conservative Christian leaders kept their distance. Dr. Dobson endorsed Senator Ted Cruz.

Since Mr. Trump clinched the nomination in May, some of those leaders have rallied to him, including Ralph Reed.

In his interview, Dr. Dobson conceded that Mr. Trump did not exactly fit the typical mold of an evangelical. "He used the word 'hell' four or five times," he said. "He doesn't know our language." He added that Mr. Trump "refers a lot to religion and not much to faith and belief."

For evangelicals, the heart of Christianity is a faith-based dependence on God. They often contrast this with what they characterize as merely "religion," which they view as more rules and rituals-based.

A spotlight on the people reshaping our politics. A conversation with voters across the country. And a guiding hand through the endless news cycle, telling you what you really need to know.

Dr. Dobson joked that Christians should take it easy on Mr. Trump for what some might perceive as slip-ups. "You got to cut him some slack," Dr. Dobson said. "He didn't grow up like we did."

Mr. Anthony referred to the Damascus-road conversion of Saul, a zealous Pharisee, who later became the Apostle Paul: "He didn't know the language either." Dr. Dobson agreed. "I think there's hope for him," Dr. Dobson said. "And I think there's hope for us."

Here is the link to the website that the above article is based on:https://www.couragematters.com/exclusive-interview-with-dr-james-dobson-did-donald-trump-recently-accept-christ/

"Put on the full armor of God, so that you will be able to stand firm against the schemes of the devil."

CHAPTER TWELVE

/ Let us guard against all the deceivers and misinformation out there

Let us realize two things here. One is that the Q posts are also being read by those on earth who are part of the Deep State, as those that President Trump and the Q team are looking at bringing to justice! What this means then is that we can be sure that they will be doing all they can, on the one hand, of seeking to show to the public that Q and the Q movement are but a conspiracy theory; and on the other hand, will be trying to divide the Q movement. For time and again patriots are reminded in the Q posts that 'united you are strong and divided you are weak.' So we should expect that the Deep State will start their own YouTube channels and websites to put out false information on either President Trump or on those involved with the Q movement, with the goal being to divide and sow seeds of doubt in the minds of those in the Q movement. I have personally gone to a few sites where I did not realize until afterwards that they were 'plants' by the Deep State, which were there only to deceive and lead one astray who is trying to follow in the Q movement.

The other thing that we need to realize here, especially those who are believers in the Q movement, is that the devil is full of schemes that he has been honing his skills at and trying out over thousands of years, where he will do whatever is necessary to try to prevent people from knowing the truth, which in this case is the truth regarding the Deep State (which we need to remember is but the visible expression on earth of the devil's plan in time for world domination) that President Trump and Q are attempting to expose through the Q posts. Therefore, it is imperative that one go in search of deciphers of the Q posts on the internet with open eyes, being mindful at all times of what has been pointed out in this chapter!

And one final note, which Q has also mentioned at least once in the Q posts, which is the fact that some deciphers are out there only for the money. In other words, let us be aware that some people have pretended to be Q followers by setting up a website and/or YouTube channel for the purpose of giving information, but in reality only did so in order to make a buck. Their true intent was not to be part of the 'Great Awakening,' but rather they saw this as an opportunity to make some money off the movement. And in having said that, we also need to keep in mind that almost all YouTube channels have advertisements, due to the fact that some of the deciphers are doing this on a full time basis and so need the financial support in order to pay expenses, which is understandable. But we still need discernment in whom we decide to support, if any.

"for it is disgraceful even to speak of the things which are done by them in secret."

Ephesians 5:12

CHAPTER THIRTEEN

/ Let us guard against going on every rabbit trail and down every rabbit hole

In this chapter, we will be discussing two things which believers should guard against while being part of the Q movement. The reality is that Q is exposing the things done in secret by the Deep State, which are of course not only sinful, but often Satanic, which means that as believers we are being exposed to what is in effect filth and mindboggling horror! And so, the two things to guard against are going on every rabbit trail and down every rabbit hole!

1) Beware of the rabbit trails

If one has ever been in the bush and tried to follow a rabbit, one soon discovers that it goes in every which direction, not sticking to any clearly defined path. The same can happen as part of the Q movement. Let me mention two of them that I have seen so far, and have quickly discarded. The one rabbit trail is the question of whether John F Kennedy Jr is still alive or not. There are many websites and YouTube channels out to prove that he is still alive.

For those who may not be aware, JFK Jr was the son of President John F Kennedy. He was three years old when his father was assassinated in Dallas in November 1963. He went on to become a lawyer, journalist, and magazine publisher. The official story is that he died in a small plane that he was flying, when it crashed on July 16, 1999, also killing his wife and her sister. Some of those involved on this rabbit trail are also out to prove that the crash was no accident. However, the reality is that on Q post #2611 of December 12, 2018, an anon asked Q if JFK Jr was still alive, and Q answered 'no,' as shown below:

JFK Jr. is Not Alive 2611
Q !!mG7VJxZNCI 12 Dec 2018 - 4:47:54 PM
Anonymous 12 Dec 2018 - 4:44:01 PM
>>4280189
Is JFK Jr alive?
>>4280260
No.
Q

What that means then is that this subject, if one continues to follow it, only leads on a rabbit trail, which really does not accomplish anything. If the plane crash was not an accident, but the plane was tampered with in a some way, thereby making this three murders, then we should wait for Q to disclose that information, which will surely come to light.

A second rabbit trail that I have noticed is whether Vice President Mike Pence is a traitor or a patriot, with there being quite a number of sites out to prove that he is a traitor. As with the above rabbit trail, I also looked at some of the evidence here also, and then dropped this rabbit trail when I discovered on the Qmap players Mike Pence is listed as patriot.

2) Beware of going down the rabbit holes

On the other hand, a rabbit hole involves one going underground, that is, below the surface to see what lies or lurks below. What is involved here is the pedophilia (sex acts with underage children), child sacrifices, human trafficking, and Satanic rituals. Again, there are many sites dedicated to these topics, especially since Q started exposing these networks and people operating on a worldwide scale. For instance, let us note Q post #29 of November 1, 2017:

North Korea Not Run by Kim 29

Anonymous 1 Nov 2017 - 12:13:10 AM

Some things must remain classified to the very end. NK is not being run by Kim, he's an actor in the play. Who is the director? The truth would sound so outrageous most Americans would riot, revolt, reject, etc.

The pedo networks are being dismantled.

The child abductions for satanic rituals (ie Haiti and other 3rd world countries) are paused (not terminated until players in custody).

We pray every single day for God's guidance and direction as we are truly up against pure evil.

And then let us note Q post #1572 of June 20th, 2018:

Sheila Jackson Lee Part of the Pedo/Satanist Club 1572

Q !CbboFOtcZs 20 Jun 2018 - 8:21:46 AM

Anonymous 20 Jun 2018 - 8:17:59 AM

ring.jpg

>>1828504

Have a peek at her ring. Just sick

>>1828594

Part of the club.

Q

And so, as believers, it is one thing to learn about all this from the Q posts and those deciphering the Q posts on various internet sites, but it is another thing to be seeking this evil stuff out, in terms of wanting to see it for ourselves, which would not serve any good purpose whatsoever. In other words, Q's goal is to let us know that this evil exists, who the people involved in it are, and that these are all being arrested, with the children involved (if still alive) being freed, which should make us rejoice and thank God. But let us not be so morbid as to seek this stuff out!

"And do not be conformed to this world, but be transformed by the renewing of your mind, so that you may prove what the will of God is, that which is good and acceptable and perfect."

Romans 12:2

"Therefore be careful how you walk, not as unwise men but as wise, making the most of your time, because the days are evil."

Ephesians 5:15,16

CHAPTER FOURTEEN

/ Let us develop a Biblical world view

For the believer, a Biblical worldview is seeing the world as God sees it, and which has God as the central Figure; which is in contrast to the worldview of an unbeliever, which is seeing the world without God being involved at all, where self is the central figure! Then the question for the believer becomes: How do we go about developing a Biblical worldview? And the answer is given by God at Romans 12:2, which is the quote to begin this chapter, "And do not be conformed to this world, but be transformed by the renewing of your mind, so that you may prove what the will of God is, that which is good and acceptable and perfect."

To "be conformed to this world" is what a person does, who does not have a Biblical worldview, whether an unbeliever, or a believer who has not yet been taught in this regard. Then God goes on to tell us as believers 'how' we are to develop a Biblical worldview, which is to "be transformed by the renewing of your mind." And so, as we read God's word daily, we are seeing how God views the world, and bit by bit our minds are being transformed to see the world as God sees it. So the key here is God's word, the Bible. As we take in God's word as our spiritual food on a daily basis, we start to think, feel, and act in ways that are in accordance with God's word, simply because we are being transformed, in both heart and mind by God's Holy Spirit within to act, speak, think, and feel as God Himself does!

But not only that; for as God continues and says, "so that we may prove what the will of God is, that which is good and acceptable and perfect," so that in having a Biblical worldview, we also learn what God's will is for believers while here on earth, which we can be sure is never something that we will ever be disappointed with or complain about! So as God says in that other quote from Ephesians 5:15,16, with which we also started this chapter, the days are indeed evil, so how important that we have a Biblical worldview in these last days, being wise and not foolish, doing God's will while here, which God has designed for our blessing and His glory!

" Rejoice always; pray without ceasing; in everything give thanks; for this is God's will for you in Christ Jesus."

1 Thessalonians 5:16-18

CHAPTER FIFTEEN

/ Let us not forget to pray!

Prayer is simply communicating with God, which is why He gave us a human spirit, so that once we have come into a personal relationship with God in salvation, He becomes our Heavenly Father and speaks to us as His child through His Son by His Holy Spirit in our human spirit. So when we pray, we are showing our dependence on God our Father for all our needs while here on earth, same as we were totally depended upon our parents when we were young living under their roof. Let us note what God discloses to us at James 1:17 about Himself, "Every good thing given and every perfect gift is from above, coming down from the Father of lights, with whom there is no variation or shifting shadow." This means our health, our finances, and everything else that might touch our lives comes from God's Hand of provision!

And so, once we have developed a Biblical worldview, and are living in accordance with that worldview, we will also be aware of what God's will is in these evil times, with part of that will being to pray, not only for our own needs, but also for the needs of those around us. And as we become involved in the Q movement, having had our eyes opened even more to how evil this world in unbelief really is, we will have a heightened sense of needing God even more, which will bring us to our knees as never before. We should at the same time become aware of just how close we are to the end of the present third age of time, which should also lead us to pray for the salvation of those God places on our path and on our hearts, and especially pray for those believers in leadership and for our families.

Then as we come to realize just how key President Trump and his administration is to standing against these evil forces at work in this world, we should be praying for President Trump, his family and his administration. Let us note the following video as an encouragement for us to do so: https://www.youtube.com/watch?v=N7k8oNhRfTw

Let us now close this chapter by noting what God has presently led His servant to pray for President Trump, his family, and his administration each morning, "Precious Father, we lift up President Trump, his wives, their children and their families to You this morning, including his cabinet and their families, his administration, staff, counselors, and advisers and their families, praying for the salvation of any who does not know You, and also for their protection. We pray especially that You would grant President Trump and his administration the guidance, wisdom, strength, and health with humbleness that is required to carry out your will in these last days. We pray that You would uphold President Trump by Your grace and grant him Your peace in the midst of continual opposition. We also ask You to tear down all fortresses that stand opposed to President Trump and his administration from all quarters, from inside the government itself; from Congress, both House and Senate; from a rogue Judiciary; from a fake mainstream media, from companies that would suppress the truth and try to prevent it from reaching the general population; and also from other countries around the world that would stand opposed. We also ask You to bring to justice all those who have broken the law, asking for the salvation of these people. We give thanks for all You have already done, praying in the Name of Your precious Son, our Lord Jesus Christ. Amen."

And just as a closing point of information, the tearing down of all fortresses in the above prayer is in accordance with what God tells us at 2 Corinthians 10:3-6, where we read, "For though we walk in the flesh, we do not war according to the flesh, for the weapons of our warfare are not of the flesh, but divinely powerful for the destruction of fortresses. We are destroying speculations and every lofty thing raised up against the knowledge of God, and we are taking every thought captive to the obedience of Christ, and we are ready to punish all disobedience, whenever your obedience is complete."

"For I am confident of this very thing, that He who began a good work in you will perfect it until the day of Christ Jesus."

Philippians 1:6

"for it is God who is at work in you, both to will and to work for His good pleasure."

Philippians 2:13

CHAPTER SIXTEEN

/ Let us go on living!

What is meant by going on living here is that we need to continue with our obligations while here on earth, to God, to family, to our employer/employees, to our community, and to country. In other words, let us not get so wrapped up with Q and the Q movement that we neglect our other obligations, for that would definitely not be God's will for us. But what we all need is wisdom and guidance from God in how to incorporate the information provided by Q into our daily lives. That is, we need to ask God what He would have us do in light of this information and in light of the fact that we are near to the end of the present age.

In the first few days after coming in contact with this information from Q, it will for sure take up quite a bit of our time, which is normal, since we are having our eyes opened to so much truth all at once that had previously been hidden from us all. However, as time goes on, we should be incorporating all of this into our daily routine as we seek to carry out our obligations. At the moment, I am at the point where I check daily if there are any new Q posts on the Qmap. If there are, I read those and then download the X22 Report for further help on deciphering those Q posts, since they would be providing some additional background information that I do have the time to look into.

"To grant us that we, being rescued from the hand of our enemies, might serve Him without fear, in holiness and righteousness before Him all our days."

Luke 1:74,75

CHAPTER SEVENTEEN

/ A last word

As we come to this last chapter, there are two things that I have becomes aware of that has really touched me so far, which were discovered since becoming involved with President Trump, Q, and the Q movement. The one relates to President George W Bush and the other to President Donald J Trump. These are the only two Presidents that I have closely followed, both during their campaigns for the Presidency, and then during their Presidency. One of these men has been a tremendous disappointment and the other a great encouragement (so far).

1) George W Bush, 43rd President of the United States

On December 13, 1999, in a Presidential debate in Iowa, George W Bush shocked me – as I was watching this live – when he declared, without even being asked as part of a question by the moderators, that he believed in Jesus Christ, and that He had changed his heart! As a believer, I was of course very thrilled, although somewhat surprised to hear that. From that moment onward, George W Bush and his family were in my prayers daily and remained so for the duration of his Presidency.

Then in 2008, I came across a book about George W Bush written by David Aikman, who was a former correspondent of Time, which was titled, "A man of faith: The spiritual journey of George W Bush." Here is what I wrote in the inside cover in June 2008 after finishing reading the book, "Very good book! Especially good to obtain the conviction from this book that President Bush is truly a child of God! Without a doubt!" And that personal opinion of George W Bush remained with me, at least until I became aware of the Q posts in 2018.

What is meant here is that I have discovered things through the Q posts that has made me greatly disappointed with George W Bush. For one thing, on the Qmap list of players, I discovered that George W Bust is listed as a traitor to his country! There is no other information given there as to the reason why. However, in reading the Q posts and then listening to many deciphers of the Q posts, it became crystal clear that President Bush #43 was very much part of the Deep State and that the September 11, 2001, attacks on the United States occurred during his watch, which many from around the world believe was an inside job, meaning that it was carried out with the knowledge of the Federal government! In any case, we still do not know for sure why George W Bush has been labeled as a traitor, but just the fact that he has been called such by Q, and that he is definitely part of the Deep State, leads me to be terribly disappointed with this man, wondering within myself how he could be a true believer and do such things!

2) Donald J Trump, 45th President of the United States

And now we will conclude as we started, that is, by talking about President Trump. Although the man has not come out publicly and claimed outright that he was a believer in The Lord Jesus Christ, nevertheless his actions so far since 2015 have shown him to be genuine, in terms of earning our trust based on carrying out all that he said he was going to do. At Matthew 12:34, God's Son told His followers in part, "the mouth speaks out of that which fills the heart." And in having observed and listened to President Trump since the election, I am amazed at how he can remain gracious toward his enemies in the face of a constant barrage of lies about him, his family, and his administration; plus being faced with a never ending list of people who oppose him, even in his own party!

So in closing the book, I must state that my greatest encouragement, apart from God Himself, has been President Trump. How encouraged I am as I follow the Q posts, as part of the Q movement, and to read over and over again in the comment section of site after site, "I am praying for President Trump," "May God bless President Trump," and "We love our President." When was the last time any of us have ever encountered such genuine outpouring of support and affection for any President! All I can say is, may God continue to protect him, for even though Q has told us that there is a plan for after Trump, there is in reality only one Trump! So let us enjoy the moment as we await as believers the soon return of our precious Lord and Savior, Jesus Christ, "Who gave Himself for our sins so that He might rescue us from this present evil age, according to the will of our God and Father, to whom be the glory forevermore. Amen."

To God alone be all praise, honor, and glory, with thanksgiving, both now and forevermore! Amen, amen, and amen.

ADDENDUM A

/ The four ages of time

What is important to know when reading God's word, the Bible, is that God has divided time into four ages. And since God's word covers all of time, then all of God's word, the Bible, can be subdivided along the lines of these four ages. But before noting what these four ages are, we need to also be aware that in each of the four ages of time, God uses the believers of that age as His vessels. In other words, God is accomplishing His work on earth through the believers of each age of time. And what is also important to keep in mind in regards to this is that although God starts each age with believers, before long the number of unbelievers in each age outnumbers the number of believers. In other words, one characteristic of each age of time is that there is a believing remnant among a mass of unbelievers, with these believers in each age being those whom God preserves for Himself and through whom God works to accomplish His purposes in each age through time.

And so in **the first age of time**, God worked through Adam and his believing descendants as His vessels to accomplish His will on earth, which age covers the first eleven chapters of Genesis. What this means is that they were the believers who willingly served Him out of love for Him. In other words, this was the believing line of descent, or the believing remnant, through which God worked out His will. Then when we begin Genesis 12, we see God take one believer, Abraham, and out of that one man's descendants through the line of Isaac, and then through the line of Jacob, God makes a nation, which is Israel. And again, we need to see that only the believing line of descent within the nation of Israel was the remnant through which God worked to accomplish His will. What this means is that not all those who were of the nation of Israel were believers. In fact, the majority were unbelievers. Therefore, in **the second age of time**, which goes from Genesis 12 to the end of Malachi in the Old Testament, and includes the gospel accounts of Matthew, Mark, Luke, and John, plus Acts 1 and Revelation 6 to 19 in the New Testament, God works out His will in time through the believers of the nation of Israel, which is again a small number compared to the total number.

And here we need to pause for a moment and mention something else before going on to consider the third age of time, and this is the fact of representation. What this means is that in the first age of time, we have Adam and Eve as our first parents, who were but representative of all people on earth. In other words, God knew that what this one couple did, any other couple would have done the same thing had they been in their place, since God knows that once sin entered His perfect and sinless creation, we all would have the same sinful nature as human beings.

Then the same is true in regards to the nation of Israel in the second age of time, in that God knew that what this one nation did, any other nation on earth would likewise have done had it been chosen by God as a representative nation. So when God set out to make the one nation of Israel, He started out with just believers. But when the nation of Israel came into existence later, only a believing remnant within the nation were believers. Now since the nation of Israel was but representative of all the nations, then God knew that if He had chosen any other nation on earth, He would find that only a believing remnant would ever become believers to serve Him willingly out of love for Him out of a mass of unbelievers who would not in any of those nations also. In other words, no other human being would have acted any differently than our first parents, and likewise, no other nation would have acted any differently than the nation of Israel did. This means that all human beings and all nations are likewise guilty before God.

What also needs to be mentioned here as we now go on to look at the third age of time, is that the first two ages basically cover the time period covered by the Old Testament, which means that the remaining third and fourth ages of time must be covered by the New Testament portion of God's word, the Bible. And let us recall that in the first age, God worked through the believers of that age, beginning with Adam, while in the second age of time, God worked through the believers of the nation of Israel, beginning with Abraham. So as we come to **the third age of time**, which goes from Acts 2 to the end of Revelation 5 in God's word, the Bible, we have God working through the believers of earth, whom God calls "the church."

What this means then is that in this third age of time, which we are presently still in, God is accomplishing His will through all the believers of earth, with God now not looking at any specific nation in particular. In other words, during the present third age of time, also known as the church age, the nation of Israel, although being supernaturally preserved by God, is still just the same as any other nation on earth, having a believing remnant among a majority of unbelievers.

Then in **the fourth age of time**, which is basically covered by Revelation 20 to 22 in the New Testament, although mentioned often in prophecy in various portions of the Old Testament, we have God working through the believers of that age, but now with much greater variation. In other words, during the fourth age of time God works through the believers of every nation on earth still in their natural bodies, and also through the believers of the first three ages of time, who would have experienced their part in the first resurrection relating to believers and who are now in their resurrected bodies. This is covered in much greater detail in my book, "An Introduction To The New World That Is Coming Upon The Earth," which focuses on this fourth age of time. If there are any readers who are not sure of what is meant by the first and second resurrection and the fact of people serving God

215

in their new resurrected bodies in the future, please see my book, "Have You Ever Wondered What Happens After Death?"

Before leaving this Addendum, it is also important to be aware that the Old Testament portion of God's word, the Bible, contains 39 books, which deal with **the beginning of all things** in God's plan of the ages, while the New Testament portion of God's word, the Bible, contains 27 books, which deal with **the consummation of all things** in God's eternal plan, which God is outworking through the four ages of time. Also of great value is knowing that the second age of time is not completed until AFTER the completion of the present third age of time. In other words, there are seven years remaining in the second age of time dealing with the nation of Israel, which is why this nation is being supernaturally preserved by God during this present third age, simply because God is not yet finished outworking His plan of the ages through that nation. This seven years remaining is a time of God's judgment against all unbelievers of earth and is approximately covered by Revelation 6:1 to Revelation 19:21 in God's word, although also mentioned often in prophecy in the Old Testament.

What also needs to be mentioned and is important to remember is that the reason God has a series of ages in time is in order to show us just how sinful the human race is and just how incapable it is of doing good, in terms of pleasing God on its own apart from God. What is meant here is that God's revelation of Himself increases as time progresses, so that those living in the fourth age of time as compared to the first age of time will have a far greater knowledge of God. In other words, as each age progresses, God makes it easier and easier for human beings on earth to come to know Him and to serve Him out of love for Him. For example, in the first two ages, God's precious Son had not yet come to earth, so that He was represented only through types, such as the animal sacrifices, the offerings, and in prophecy. Human beings at that time also only had the Old Testament as light to guide them.

But by the time we reach the fourth age of time, God's precious Son will not only have come from Heaven to earth bodily, but will actually be on earth reigning over the nations as King. Please note what God says at Isaiah 11:9 in part, as just one example, "...For the earth will be full of the knowledge of the Lord as the waters cover the sea." What this means then is that when God's final judgment of time comes, relating to all the unbelievers of time (Revelations 20:11-15), then none of these unbelievers of time will be able to stand before God and give any excuse for their sin of unbelief, in having personally and freely rejected God's offer of salvation found in His own precious Son, The Lord Jesus Christ. And so each succeeding age adds to mankind's culpability before a Holy and altogether Righteous God so that in the end "every mouth may be closed and all the world may become accountable to God" (Romans 3:19 in part).

ADDENDUM B

/ The two comings from Heaven to earth of God's precious Son, our Lord Jesus Christ

Another very important truth to know here is that God's word, the Bible, mentions **two comings** of God's precious Son, Jesus Christ, from Heaven to earth. His **first coming** from Heaven to earth was for the purpose of taking on a body like ours, only in the innocence of Adam and as born of a virgin so as not to incur our sinful nature, and then after living thirty-three and half years on earth carrying out only the will of God His Father in absolute sinlessness out of love for Him, was given over into the hands of unbelievers to be put to death on a cross, before being buried, then resurrected from the dead the third day. And of course, His death was not due to anything God's precious Son, The Lord Jesus Christ, had ever done wrong, but rather was to pay the penalty due the sins of the human race, which was death, in order that God might have a basis by which to forgive the sins of those who believe in Him.

Then **the second coming** of God's precious Son is to be seen as being **in two stages**. The **first stage** of His second coming is at the end of this present third age of time, and is for the purpose of bringing to Heaven all believers of earth before God's judgment falls on the unbelievers of the earth, thereby bringing the present third age to a close. God has this first stage in view especially at 1 Thessalonians 4:14-17, although also mentioned in many portions of the New Testament. Then the **second stage** of the second coming of

God's precious Son, The Lord Jesus Christ, occurs at the end of the seven years remaining of the second age of time. God's precious Son would now be coming to bring judgment on all unbelievers of earth of the present time, before establishing His reign on earth as King during the fourth age of time. This is again disclosed by God in many portions of God's word in the New Testament, but especially in passages such as Matthew 24:29,30 and Revelation 19:11-21. Therefore, as we next turn to look at the subject matter of this book proper it is good to remember all that we have just looked at in Addendum A and B as background information and as a foundation for what we are now going to look at in the book.

"Jesus said to him, "I am the way, and the truth, and the life; no one comes to the Father but through Me."
"

John 14:6

ADDENDUM C

/ For those who may not as yet know God in a personal relationship

Possibly you have been reading this book and have become aware of not knowing this God Who created us and gave us physical life into this world, and up to now has allowed you to live on earth. However, you do have the desire to know God in a personal way. If this is the case, then this chapter has been written specifically for you. And what God wants you to have in coming to know Him is the peace and joy which comes in knowing that all of your sins committed in your lifetime are forgiven and that you have eternal life with God. And so, your greatest need at the moment is to make peace with God so as to go to Heaven, which is God's eternal home. And so this chapter will help to bring that about by pointing you to God's Son, The Lord Jesus Christ, so as to come to personally know God through faith in His Son.

And as we begin, we need to note a most important promise which God makes at Romans 6:23 to all those who do not yet know Him, "**For the wages of sin is death, but the free gift of God is eternal life in Christ Jesus our Lord.**" The good news here is that God offers you eternal life with Him as a free gift, which is to be obtained in His Son, Jesus Christ. What God does not do in this verse from the Bible is tell us 'how' to obtain that eternal life with Him. Another verse which we can look at where God does let us know 'how' one can obtain that eternal life with Him is noting what God tells us at John 3:16, "**For God so loved the world, that He gave His**

223

only begotten Son, that whoever believes in Him shall not perish, but have eternal life." Now the added truth which God makes known here is that the eternal life, which He gives to a human being as a free gift, is for those who believe in His Son.

Then the question is: What is it that I am to **believe** about God's Son, Jesus Christ, which will lead God to give me eternal life with Him forever? And the beauty of God is that He never leaves us guessing, especially when it comes to having a personal relationship with Him, which He desires us to have. Therefore, we should not be surprised when God gives us the answer to our question in what He tells us at 1 Corinthians 15:1-4, "[1] Now I make known to you, brethren, **the gospel** which I preached to you, which also you received, in which also you stand, [2] **by which also you are saved**, if you hold fast the word which I preached to you, unless you believed in vain. [3] For I delivered to you as of first importance what I also received, that **Christ died for our sins** according to the Scriptures, [4] **and that He was buried, and that He was raised on the third day** according to the Scriptures…"

Therefore, "the gospel," which simply means 'good news,' which God wants you to hear and believe in order to "be saved," which simply refers to you coming to know God and have eternal life with Him, is that His Son has already died for you, has already been buried, and has already been raised from the dead again the third day after His death, and Has now ascended back to Heaven again in order that God would have a basis by which to forgive you of all your sins, which are all against Him, and to freely give you eternal life with Him, for simply believing this message in your heart.

One thing which often prevents a person from believing the gospel at this point is not seeing oneself as **a sinner before a Holy God**. When we look at ourselves by our own assessment, and especially when we compare ourselves with others around us, we often think of ourselves as being better than others, and so good enough to enter Heaven in our present condition. The problem with this is that it is the product of our own thinking and is not God's assessment of our situation. God's assessment of our situation is as He tells us at Romans 3:10-12,23 in part, "[10] as it is written, "There is **none righteous**, not even one… [11] there is none who seeks for God [12] all have turned aside… there is none who does good, there is not even one... [23] for **all have sinned** and fall short of the glory of God…""

This is quite a different assessment of the human race from that which we as human beings often have of ourselves, is this not? But why would God have such an assessment of the whole human race? For the answer to that question, we need to be aware that God is Creator of all that exists, so that when God created the first man, Adam, at the beginning of time, God created him in **innocence**, meaning that Adam as first created by God neither knew good nor evil, nor was there any sin anywhere in God's original sinless creation.

However, the day came when **God tested Adam with a command**, saying to him in the garden of Eden here on earth, which was the perfect environment which God had for him, what we now read at Genesis 2:16,17, "The Lord God commanded the man, saying, "From any tree of the garden you may eat freely; [17] but from the tree of the knowledge of good and evil you shall not eat, for in the day that you eat from it you will surely **die**." How important to see here that God gave Adam, who although a real person was also representative of the whole human race, the warning of **the penalty of death for disobedience to His command.**

Unfortunately, the day did come when Adam did partake of the forbidden tree and thereby did sin against God. The moment that happened, Adam not only became a sinner by practice, but also **a sinner by nature.** One thing my parents had to continually do while under their care was to restrain me from continually going the wrong way, for it seemed that of myself I could not do good, but kept going into sin. The reason this was happening is that from the age of accountability onwards, I had not only become a sinner by practice, but also a sinner by nature. And here the age of accountability needs to be seen as being when as a young child in innocence - which moment is known only by God - one comes to learn the right from the wrong and chooses the wrong, thereby becoming personally accountable to God for one's own sin against Him, since all sin is first of all against Him. And that is why God can say at Romans 3:23 above that "all have sinned and fall short of the glory of God," because God knows that all human beings will go the way of Adam, our representative man, which is also why God can say what He does in regards to the whole of the human race at Romans 5:12, where we read, "Therefore, just as through one man (Adam) sin entered into the world, and death through sin, and **so death spread to all men, because all sinned**" (from the age of accountability onward).

And so we see that the whole human race is declared by God to not only be sinners by practice and by nature from the age of accountability onwards, but the whole of the human race is now subject to death! In other words, in God's sight the whole of the human race is under the judgment of the penalty of death, due to all being sinners by practice and by nature. You will recall above, in the first verse we quoted from Romans 6:23, God did say there that "the wages of sin is death." And what God means by "death" here is not just loss of physical life, when the physical body we have dies, but also has spiritual death in mind, which is far worse! Spiritual death has its beginning when a separation takes place between a person and God at the moment one becomes a sinner at the age of accountability and ends after the final judgment of time, when God forever casts away from His Presence those who before physical death refused to believe in His Son, Jesus Christ, thereby personally forfeiting the forgiveness of their sins and eternal life with God. And now all such will pay the penalty for their own sins in **hell**, away from the Presence of God forever.

It is in the midst of such a hopeless situation in which the whole of the human race found itself in that **GOD TOOK THE INITIATIVE** and sent His own eternally existing Son into the world, as born of a virgin in the innocence of Adam – so as not to inherit the sinful nature passed on from generation after generation from Adam onwards – so that He might be the acceptable sacrifice offered to God His Father at the cross, there bearing our sins in His body, and there dying the death due our sins! God's Son, Jesus Christ, was then buried and raised from the dead the third day, to ever be alive, for it is through Him, on the basis of what God has done for us through His Son, that God The Father forgives our sins and imparts us eternal life.

Now, by God's grace and His enablement, may you see your need of God's Son to be Your Savior from the penalty due sin, which is death, not only physical, but also spiritual. And by God's grace, may He lead you to believe in His Son, Jesus Christ, and in believing, to **receive the forgiveness of your sins and eternal life with Him forever!** And based on the truth just shared, I would now like to ask you a few questions, with the answer being just between yourself and God:

When God says at Romans 3:23, "for all have sinned and fall short of the glory of God," does that include you?

When God says at Romans 5:8, "But God demonstrates His own love toward us, in that while we were yet sinners, Christ died for us," were you included in Christ's death on behalf of sinners?

And when God further says at 1 Peter 3:18 in part, "For Christ also died for sins once for all, the just for the unjust, so that He might bring us to God, having been put to death in the flesh, but made alive in the spirit," were you part of the unjust for whom Christ died?

When God says at Romans 6:23, "For the wages of sin is death, but the free gift of God is eternal life in Christ Jesus our Lord," do you want that eternal life as a free gift from God?

When God says at John 3:16, "For God so loved the world, that He gave His only begotten Son, that whoever believes in Him shall not perish, but have eternal life," do you now believe that Jesus Christ is indeed God's Son in human flesh, Who came from Heaven to this earth to die in your place, so as to save you from ever experiencing the judgment of God leading to an eternal separation from God in hell?

And when God then further says to you at Isaiah 55:6, "Seek the Lord while He may be found; call upon Him while He is near," for His further promise to you here is as we read at Romans 10:9-11,13, "[9] that if you confess with your mouth Jesus as Lord, and believe in your heart that God raised Him from the dead, you will be saved (that is, you will now enter into a personal relationship with God by faith); [10] for with the heart a person believes, resulting in righteousness (that is, in now receiving God's own righteous eternal life to live by), and with the mouth he confesses, resulting in salvation (that is, in now receiving as a free gift the forgiveness of sins and eternal life with God). [11] For the Scripture says, "Whoever believes in Him will not be disappointed..." [13] for "Whoever will call on the name of the Lord will be saved." **Will you now call upon God from your heart, telling God in your own words your answer to each question that has just been asked?**

My prayer for you at this point, as you now call upon God by His grace, is what we read at Romans 15:13, "**Now may the God of hope fill you with all joy and peace in believing**, so that you will abound in hope by the power of the Holy Spirit."

ADDENDUM D

/ Useful Resources

Please note that all video links were active at the time the book was published. If for some reason a link is not active – which could be because a video has been removed by YouTube, for example – then please do a search on one of the following conservative and uncensored alternative sites that have sprung up:

https://www.bitchute.com/

https://www.altcensored.com/

https://drop.space/

Chapter 1:

Trump campaign video:

https://www.youtube.com/watch?v=G2qIXXafxCQ

US military video:

https://www.youtube.com/watch?v=zCqKnqMqIhI

The White House website:

https://www.whitehouse.gov

Chapter 2:

My preferred site for Q posts:

https://qmap.pub

https://qalerts.app/

https://qagg.news/

https://qanon.pub/

https://qanon.news/Q/

Q Research board:

https://8ch.net/qresearch/index.html

X22 Report:

https://www.youtube.com/user/X22Report/videos?app=desktop

In Pursuit Of Truth (IPOT):

https://www.youtube.com/channel/UCAyrKoW31y5UcsRjh2ItvxQ/videos

The White House website:

https://www.whitehouse.gov

President Trump's personal website:

https://www.donaldjtrump.com

Chapter 3:

No video links.

Chapter 4:

Video link 'Who controls our money?'

https://www.youtube.com/watch?v=mQUhJTxK5mA

United Nations system chart:

http://www.un.org/en/pdfs/18-00159e_un_system_chart_17x11_4c_en_web.pdf

Video link to "Who made MD's King:"

https://www.youtube.com/watch?v=blxeEHV1Iio

Video link to "Cancer: The forbidden cures:"

https://www.youtube.com/watch?v=zmQZcj3CggI

Video link to 'The Bohemian Grove: The most forbidden place in America:'
https://www.youtube.com/watch?v=5UM3KbmfoG4

Video link to 'American under siege, the Deep State:'

https://www.youtube.com/watch?v=6YUcUoFveJc

Video link to 'Qanon, killing the mockingbird media:'

https://www.youtube.com/watch?v=AHS0UjpM9sE

Video link to, 'The beast system revealed'

https://www.youtube.com/watch?v=21qZUBoLr0U

Video link to, 'They are preparing us for the prince of darkness'

https://www.youtube.com/watch?v=m8HLq4zWq4s

Video link to, 'Biblical beast system rapidly rising'

https://www.youtube.com/watch?v=VVULi9iRHMw

Video link to, 'Unknowingly giving life to the beast system:'

https://www.youtube.com/watch?v=X4BN__QbvZQ

Video link to, 'The A.I. takeover is here!,'

https://www.youtube.com/watch?v=X8ovlix5fNl

Video link to, 'The scary future of America, 2019-2020'

https://www.youtube.com/watch?v=VP-yweVg2q4

Chapter Five:

Video link to, 'We are the plan:'

https://www.youtube.com/watch?v=MRtEgdgj_XQ&list=PL3G
PDGjW5SiOnzyvONdfODbjSgZ136nEZ

Chapter Six:

Video link to, 'The 2nd American revolution is underway:'

https://www.youtube.com/watch?v=j1rjiJgM8_g

Chapter Seven:

Video link to movie trailer, 'White Squall:'

https://www.youtube.com/watch?v=B5T7Gr5oJbM&feature=y
outu.be

Video link to song by J.T. Wilde, 'WWG1WGA:'

https://www.youtube.com/watch?v=KXNiBMlxl7g

Chapter Eight:

No video links.

Chapter nine:

No video links.

Chapter Ten:

No video links.

Chapter Eleven:

Video link to, 'Recognizing God's Hand in Trump's election:

https://www.youtube.com/watch?v=aRcnJPQqY0c

Video link to President Trump standing for religious freedom
and Biblical values:

https://www.youtube.com/watch?v=FWTQgl4VSEY

https://www.youtube.com/watch?v=HmmW6Q1oLfM

Video links to where President Trump asks someone to pray before starting a meeting at the White House:

https://www.youtube.com/watch?v=DQDzCbAHwFY

https://www.youtube.com/watch?v=b4itRBfSJhM

https://www.youtube.com/watch?v=a0_mCivoTSs

Video links to where President Trump consents to have someone pray for him:

https://www.youtube.com/watch?v=US9nlaVF9ZM

https://www.youtube.com/watch?v=42nK8wo_fwE

Video link to President Trump addressing a graduating class:

https://www.youtube.com/watch?v=Rpfkh1HLsiE

Video link to source of the New York Times article:

https://www.couragematters.com/exclusive-interview-with-dr-james-dobson-did-donald-trump-recently-accept-christ/

Chapter Twelve

No video links.

Chapter Thirteen

No video links.

Chapter Fourteen

No video links.

Chapter Fifteen:

Video link to encourage believers to pray for President Trump:

https://www.youtube.com/watch?v=N7k8oNhRfTw

Chapter Sixteen:

No video links

Chapter Seventeen:

No video links.

/ The next book

As this book is being published, the next book that God has given His approval to is, "God's Consummation Of All In The Book Of Revelation," which would be the eighth book in The Word Of God Library, and which would be the author's forty-sixth published work. But in case it is not the book that is written, readers may want to stay current with the author's main website, where it will be made known if another book has been written. My main website is:

http://www.pilgrimpathwaypublications.com

And if you have enjoyed reading this book or any other of the author's books, please feel free to give me feedback at the above website, and also let family, friends, and co-workers know about this book and my other books. The author is not on any social media sites, so he relies on God and readers like you to spread the word. May God bless you for doing so.

www.ingramcontent.com/pod-product-compliance
Lightning Source LLC
Chambersburg PA
CBHW020425290526
45784CB00012BA/228